Strategic Skills for Line Managers

Strategic Skills for Line Managers

Michael Colenso

OXFORD   AUCKLAND   BOSTON   JOHANNESBURG   MELBOURNE   NEW DELHI

Butterworth-Heinemann
Linacre House, Jordan Hill, Oxford OX2 8DP
225 Wildwood Avenue, Woburn, MA 01801-2041
A division of Reed Educational and Professional Publishing Ltd

℞ A member of the Reed Elsevier plc group

First published 1998

British Library Cataloguing in Publication Data
Colenso, Michael
    Strategic skills for line managers. – (New skills
    portfolio)
    1. Strategic planning
    I. Title
    658.4'012

ISBN 0 7506 3982 2

Composition by Genesis Typesetting, Laser Quay, Rochester, Kent
Printed and bound in Great Britain

FOR EVERY TITLE THAT WE PUBLISH, BUTTERWORTH-HEINEMANN
WILL PAY FOR BTCV TO PLANT AND CARE FOR A TREE.

Contents

Series editor's preface

The last decade has seen considerable change in the world of employment. Organizations have shed roles and management layers in their attempt to be more cost-effective, competitive and closer to their customers. The 'leaner organization' concept, with its emphasis on teamworking, better use of technologies and greater opportunities for innovation, certainly appears to be benefiting many organizations which have seen improvements in quality and the bottom line. The trend towards ongoing organizational change and restructuring appears set to continue.

What appears to be successful as an organizational strategy may offer fewer benefits to employees however. Changing work practices have carried in their wake a degree of confusion. Job security cannot be taken for granted and ongoing hard work seems the order of the day. The dividing line between work and other aspects of life becomes increasingly blurred as mobile phones, e-mail, the Internet, remote conferencing means that employees are expected to be accessible anywhere, anytime. Teleworking, hot-desking and project working means that employees are expected to be largely self-managing, flexible and adaptable, able to work in teams which cross organizational boundaries and are in some cases virtual.

A key development in recent times is the increasing call for employees to manage their own careers, to think of themselves as self-employed, to upgrade their skills at the same time as holding down demanding jobs. The old 'psychological contract' by which employees might expect continuous employment and prospects of promotion up a vertical hierarchy in return for loyalty and effective performance, seems to have been replaced by the notion that employees can gain long-term security only by developing their skills and making themselves employable. Of course in the world of organized employment, there has been a buyers' market for jobs except in certain fields such as IT where limited supplies of skilled employees mean that it is the employees who hold the whip hand.

I have been carrying out research into the changing workplace, in particular the effect of flatter organization structures on careers, since 1994. This is very much in line with the mission of Roffey Park Management Institute, where I work, to investigate issues relating to the health and well-being of people at work. I have found that many people find the challenges of coping with ongoing change and constant hard work debilitating. Other people seem to have found the recipe for success and energy in this changing context. I have studied what appears to make some people cope so much more effectively with change than others do, and I have looked at some of the skills used by these individuals. It is the range of skills which enables these employees not only to survive but thrive in constantly changing organizations which is the focus of this series.

This series is intended to provide a self-help skills development resource. The authors have been selected not just because of their undoubted expertise in the subject matter of their book, but also because they can write in a way which will enable you to develop or enhance your ability in the skill in question. This is not 'just a lot of theory'. Rather, each book offers a blend of practical activities, background information and examples from organizations and individuals, which should make sense whether you are simply dipping in for the odd idea, or working through in a systematic way. The books offer a range of insights and suggestions for further learning which will be useful to the serious self-developer. They focus on the truly transferable 'meta-skills' of lifelong learning.

So whether you are a specialist who recognizes the need to develop a broader business understanding, or a generalist who sees the need to develop some real 'knowledge' skills, this series has something to offer. Books in the series address some of the key skill areas for current and future success. Based on my research, I propose that the ability to think and act strategically is vital at any level in an organization. New approaches to thinking creatively and introducing innovation will become increasingly important, as will the ability to work in a range of different types of team. Project working is becoming commonplace and the 'new' project skills are as relevant to team members as to team leaders. As the workplace continues to evolve, the ability to work effectively in a range of networks and informal groupings will be valuable.

Above all, the people who acquire the ability to manage themselves and their time, including taking responsibility for their own career, are likely to be the people who can exercise genuine choice. Knowing what you want, developing your skills and having the ability to make things happen is likely to make you truly employable. As some organizations have already found to their cost, employees whose skills are in demand are able to make their own choices rather than having to rely on their employer. Perhaps making a commitment to yourself and your development is the surest guarantee of securing what is important to you. Good luck and enjoy the journey!

Linda Holbeche
Director of Research
Roffey Park Management Institute

Introduction

For some time now I have observed the momentum which drives organizations move from the boardroom to the managers. Roles seem to be polarizing differently. Increasingly it seems to me that senior management, including the top team, is out networking, wheeling and dealing, scanning the environment, staying in touch with a wider world, and out looking for opportunity. Middle managers are left to run the shop.

It also seems that while the big change initiatives still come from the top, the organic day-to-day development and adaptation of the company is increasingly in the hands of line managers and their people. Some of this may be because more organizations than previously are operating on a model of employee empowerment. Whether from choice or necessity is harder to say.

For a whole raft of reasons the 'control models' even of the recent past are increasingly inoperable. Just for example, I think there is a strong case for suggesting that the process of agreeing and reviewing objectives, thought to be a valid means for an organization to communicate its will to its employees, is no longer necessarily achieving this intention, and may not even be in the best interest of the organization. I cannot be alone in finding that the objectives of the last quarter often seem to be largely irrelevant when the review date comes round.

In figuring out what you need to do these days to run an organization effectively, I have been engaged by the work of the general systems scientists of the 1960s and 1970s. They gave us a really effective model, a model which works because it is the product of the relentlessly unforgiving powers of evolution. The model is the human body; an inherently uncontrollable mass of functionally specific entities many, or most, of which deliver their functional benefits continuously, efficiently and without the intervention of a management system intent on issuing and agreeing objectives.

It has often been an effective means of getting my point across to retreat into the tedium of simplicity, and I hope you will allow me to develop my argument in a way which might produce apoplexy in a biologist.

The various parts of the human body deliver their functional benefits because each 'knows' very clearly what it is there to do. Not only does it know what it is specifically there to do, but it is also knows that it is part of a unique entity, a given individual. So what you have is an aggregation of expert functional systems, each performing to the unique specification of the individual, each adapting to the immediate environment, each continuing to function even if that environment becomes hostile and only demanding the attention of the boardroom/brain if it can no longer cope.

So what has this all got to do with the momentum generated by middle managers or the need to think strategically? Well here is the analogy expanded.

On the left-hand side we have the desired behaviour of the organization's component parts, on the right-hand side the biological parallel:

- All functions operate efficiently and each delivers its unique and indispensable benefit ⇨ . . . the body stays healthy

- They do so even when the environment in which they are operating is constantly changing ⇨ . . . winter, summer, at work, at leisure, playing sport, lolling on the beach

● They adapt when the conditions for their optimal performance are not delivered	⇨ . . . dealing with a hangover, lack of sleep, catching a cold
● They adapt when patterns underlying their experiences change permanently or semi permanently	⇨ . . . you gain 5 kilos in weight, you take up, or give up smoking, you train for a marathon
● They do so without asking permission, seeking additional compensation, getting it in writing	⇨ . . . i.e. without recourse to the central nervous system; without your conscious intervention

To do this all components in the organization must:

● have a very clear idea of why they are there, their fundamental purpose, the long-term view
● have a clear idea of what is expected of them as a consistent level of performance
● understand the specific nature of the organization of which they are a part
● understand the long-term intent of the organization.

These are the major components of a strategy, and what it delivers for an organization is:

● alignment within the organization of the systems and components of which it is composed to achieve its strategic intent
● appropriate, self-generated adaptation to internal and external developments, i.e. changing of their own volition in a way which is informed by, and consistent with, the strategy.

If we push the analogy as far as it will go, the strategy of the organization equates to the DNA of the body – the message in every cell which tells the cell what it is there to do and what the characteristics of its host person are.

So if we put a strategy together which is meant to work like DNA works in a living organism, what information will it have to be capable of passing on to the employees? Here is my list:

- The *purpose* of the organization.
- The *purpose* of my unit within the organization.
- The *values* of the organization – what it puts up with, what it draws the line at.
- The *values* of my unit (which had better be congruent with those of the organization or, guess what, the organization's immune system will swat us).
- The *vision* of the organization – what it is trying to become as defined by the environment in which it operates and the *purpose* it serves.
- The *vision* of my unit (which had better be congruent or, guess what . . . etc.).
- The *strategic intent* of the organization – what is its broad brush plan for achieving the *purpose*, while conforming to the *values* and delivering the *vision*.
- Ditto the unit . . . and ditto the congruence.
- The *critical success factors* – a clear idea, short and medium term, of what success looks like. How will we know, organization and unit, if we are getting there?
- The ability – the competence to do all the above.

Now there is another critical part of the analogy. You can tell the functional units all this information. Some of it will stick, some of it will not, some of what sticks will affect the behaviour of the unit, and some of what sticks will not affect its behaviour. So what this means is that a small part of what you tell the unit is actually translated into behaviour. (This leads management to adopt the earnest but often futile techniques we describe as *the management of change*.)

The body, however, i.e. the central nervous system (the board, the top team), does not use the 'tell' route at all. It uses a systemic route. In other words the critical information is part of the make-up of the component parts. They have not 'heard it', they 'know it', it is embedded, it is part of their nature, it is understood and, as a result, it influences how they behave.

How do you do it? How do you embed and make systemic the information which will produce purposeful survival directed behaviour?

There is only one way I know and that is by creating the conditions in which those whom you wish to be influenced are used in defining and creating the information which will affect their behaviour. Developing strategy is a participative activity, if it is not you lose the linkage between it and organizational behaviour.

And there is another condition, the behaviour has to be reinforced when it is appropriate and corrected when it is not. This is the core process of learning, there is no other.

So that is why I have written this book, to provide a set of strategic skills for use by line managers or indeed by anybody within the organization who has responsibility for people.

I know of no more cogent way to improve radically the behaviour of an organization than for all of it to be operating with understanding of, and constant reference to, its strategy.

Dare to do it, delight your owners, and fulfil your people.

How to use this book

The book is built in three main parts:

- Chapters 1 to 5 aim to tell you all about strategy, what it is, what it looks like when it is working and how the current operating environment of organizations is affecting it.
- Chapters 6 to 13 give you a detailed route to follow to build your own strategy whether you are working on a strategy for a whole organization, or a strategy for an operating unit, team or department of an organization.
- Chapters 14 and 15 discuss measuring and excellence respectively.

At the heart of the book lies a relatively simple philosophy of presentation:

- Explain, as briefly as possible, what the reader needs to know.
- Present an Activity which tees up some results you can use.
- Show, where relevant or possible, a case study application so that you have an example or two of how the Activity works out in reality.

If you want to talk to me try
101733.2337@compuserve.com.

Good luck!

1 Strategy: what it is and why it is important

Strategy is about winning wars. It is, quite literally, the art of generalship. At one level it is about deploying troops and resources on the battlefields of your choice, and doing so in such a way that you defeat the enemy. It is about creating the conditions which favour your victory. And it has another dimension; it is about long-term victory. The central concern of the strategist may not even be about fighting, but it is about gaining lasting supremacy.

The earliest writings on strategy are Chinese. Sun Tzu wrote *The Art of War* in 512 BC. He too recommended skipping the battle: '100 victories in 100 battles is not the pinnacle of excellence. Subjugating the enemy's army without fighting is the true pinnacle of excellence.'

So it is also about outmanoeuvring your enemy to gain supremacy and if you can do so without crossing swords, so much the better. Sun Tzu, I must add, is currently high fashion in the business community and much read.

Strategy is not simply about making a plan and sticking to it. Because the strategic environment is essentially combative in nature, it is reasonable to expect that your combatants will also be seeking victory, will also be deploying resources on their chosen battlefields, will also be in it for the long term.

This creates an inherently unstable environment in which long-term planning becomes difficult to sustain as each of you tries to outmanoeuvre the other. Compounding this instability is the fact that in a business environment there are usually several 'combatants' some of whom you may not even have recognized as such.

Responding to events in this changing environment we deploy tactics – short-term responses to unfolding events. Each tactical move must be undertaken to support the overall strategic intent. This brings us to the absolute heart of the problem; perhaps the hardest thing in the hurly-burly of changing day-to-day events is not to lose sight of the strategic intent.

Strategic intent

What is strategic intent? It is a statement or a series of statements which outline what the organization is trying to achieve in the long term. The best examples are relatively simple to comprehend though not necessarily easy to execute. Winning the Second World War, a strategic intent common to both the Allies and the Axis incidentally, is a pretty clear intent. It is simple enough for leaders to communicate unambiguously, it is important enough to hold people's attention, and the consequences of failing to achieve it are sufficiently compelling to mobilize huge effort.

Simplicity, clarity and a high degree of focused commercial aggression seem to characterize many of the most successful corporate strategies as well.

Komatsu, the highly successful Japanese earth-moving equipment manufacturer, described its strategic intent as 'encircling Caterpillar'. Caterpillar, from their famed Peoria headquarters, dominated the world's markets. Starting, as Komatsu did, with laughably inadequate resources when compared with the mighty market leader, the intent of beating Caterpillar successfully drove the Japanese company's corporate strategy for more than two decades.

Komatsu chipped away relentlessly at Caterpillar's market dominance; country by country, product line by product line, Komatsu's strategy sought to attack Caterpillar's existing position. Slowly but surely, the underresourced and technologically inferior Japanese company mobilized its resources, deployed them selectively, and ramped up its technological capability to compete eyeball to eyeball with Caterpillar.

While Caterpillar survived the onslaught, Komatsu's focused aggression has energized its workforce and enabled it to grow from a domestic Japanese manufacturer to a global player of great size and market influence.

While an A triumphs over B strategic intent most closely bridges strategy in its military sense and in its business sense, not all strategic intent is as aggressively targeted.

Apple Computer's strategic intent was 'a computer in every home'. This is a much more benign and visionary intent, and when Steve Jobs, the charismatic president of Apple, articulated it, it seemed bizarre. Computers were, for the most part, mighty machines, serviced by rafts of specialist attendants. In pursuing this strategic intent Apple transformed the environment of computing making it simpler, user friendly, intuitive and accessible.

This transformation in turn allowed the growth and dominance of Microsoft, whose strategic intent was to monopolize computer operating systems. With DOS and Windows, Microsoft has pretty nearly, though not quite, achieved this. Now, in the late 1990s, Microsoft's strategic intent is to dominate the Internet – this, too, is a strategic intent shared by more than one company.

Importantly strategic intent is aspirational; it can have either a David versus Goliath character as with Komatsu versus Caterpillar, or it can have a benign for-the-goodness-ofmankind type character as did Apple. However it is expressed, if it is to energize and stretch the employees of a company, if it is to stimulate them to exceptional performance, they must feel it is worth their effort, their time and their attention. Somehow the strategic intent must resonate with employees' values; people must wish to be a part of this grand enterprise.

To complete the circle on a topic to which we will continuously return in this book, strategic intent must be capable of clear articulation not only by the senior members of the organization, but also by all of its employees. Importantly it must inform shorter-term strategic or tactical moves, and it must consistently define the compass point by which the organization is steering.

Ownership of, and participation in, strategy

In some organizations the strategic plan is developed in a secret corporate enclave traditionally staffed by a clutch of people with MBAs. By and large this model does not work. In other organizations, developing and honing the strategy is a continuous process of collectively refining and developing ways and means of delivering the strategic intent. This latter model is usually more successful.

The Japanese system called *Hoshin Kanri* is designed to enlist the entire organization in strategy development. *Hoshin* means 'compass', *Kanri* means 'planning'. In effect, having established the strategic intent, the destination to which the organization is being steered and the compass point by which it is being steered, the whole organization participates in developing operating activities which support that direction. The strategic intent, usually illuminated by a number of critical success factors – those things which have to go right – is passed down the organization so that it undergoes continuous reality tests by the line managers. It is also tested across the organization to achieve alignment and unlock the potential for cross-functionality.

From this ongoing activity a series of relatively short-term objectives are developed usually clustered into two different categories:

- Things – products, processes, services, operating activities – on which we must improve. Here we are looking at continuous improvement, incremental development.
- Areas where we need to break through, where we must reinvent, where imagination, creativity, innovation, reconceptualization, redefinition is necessary. Here we are looking at breaking the mould.

The *Hoshin Kanri* practice is ongoing. The analogy which its proponents always offer is of the sailing-boat which must continuously change direction, tacking this way and that as it takes advantages of or compensates for the effects of winds and currents – the operating environment in other words. However, these short-term directional changes – the tactics – merely enable a steady progression towards the predetermined destination – the strategic intent.

However it is done, most organizations unsurprisingly adduce great benefit in creating among employees a sense of ownership and collective involvement in developing strategy. As a distinguished mentor of mine used to say: 'Only a plan with everybody's fingerprints on it will work.'

The line manager as strategist

While it is obvious that line manager participation will help refine, develop and ultimately implement the operating objectives needed to support the organization's strategic intent, there is another level at which the line manager must operate as strategist.

Every operating unit of an organization, every functional division, department, team or whatever it is called is a mini-organization in its own right. Each should be clear about where its competition lies and how to gain competitive advantage. Each should have a strategic intent, and each should also regard its continued existence as being dependent on being able to satisfy its customers.

Operating units will only look at themselves in this way to the extent that the line manager, supervisor or team leader provides the impetus to do so and the opportunity or space to focus members' thinking on the reason they are there. It is for this reason that line managers' ability to think and act strategically has increasingly occupied the development plans of organizations.

Research conducted by Britain's Institute of Management sought, in a survey of over 1,200 managers, to discover those skills which should be developed in line managers as they approached the millennium. A remarkable 78 per cent of respondents identified *strategic thinking* as the first priority. Definers of this skill included words like 'longer term' and 'broader perspective'.

If you have not read the Introduction to this book, I must repeat my conviction that the participation of the line manager in strategy development and execution is a key and crucial condition for the success of the organization; a critical success factor if you like. It is to help develop the skills that underpin and enable this activity that this book is written.

The last decade has seen organizations spinning off or outsourcing functions which in the past might have been regarded as key components of its strength. The success rate of these outsourced activities has been surprisingly high. One of the reasons is, I believe, that once out from under the protective and/or stultifying effect of a larger parent organization, management of the facility has been able to concentrate on really key issues:

key concept	What are we here to do?	*Strategic purpose*
	Where will we concentrate our energies so that we can deliver our purpose in the long term?	*Strategic intent*
	What has to go right to achieve our strategic intent?	*Critical success factors*
	What strengths will we have to develop to manage the organization so that we achieve our strategic intent?	*Core competencies*

The route to developing this clarity must also cover *vision*, a shared picture of what we would like to become in the future, and *values*, the rules by which we will play the game.

Clarifying these issues and achieving consensus among employees and colleagues unlocks energy and imagination as to how to run and improve the business. It produces focus on customers' needs and it tees up objectives in the areas of continuous improvement and breakthrough which we identified above. It lends to people's jobs a purpose and direction which is usually highly satisfactory.

Strategy as leadership

Before we leave this brief canter through the importance of strategy, it is important to link strategy to the concept of leadership. Leadership is a compound of a number of characteristics, some are personality or character based, some are manifest by the way people behave. Some have to do with a predisposition to action – getting on with things – and some have to do with personal beliefs and values.

Importantly, some of the characteristics of leaderships are skills based and, arguably, chief among these is the ability to think and act strategically. This book aims really to provide the line manager with some of the key tools to develop those skills. To use them is to change the way many managers, supervisors or team leaders do their jobs.

When I conduct workshops with line managers on strategy, part of my intention is to debunk the mysticism with which the subject has become surrounded – the province of those with MBAs operating, metaphorically, in the annex to the boardroom. Realizing the accessibility of the tools to all, and the value that thinking strategically provides to all employees, usually helps line managers feel more in control of their jobs.

Help screens

At the end of most of the chapters in this book is a Help Screen which summarizes as succinctly as possible the key concepts in the chapter. Reviewing the Help Screens will be a quick and easy way of recalling the content of the chapter.

Help

Strategy
- the art of generalship
- predisposing things so that you win

Strategic intent
- where we want to be/what we want to achieve
- simple, clear, unambiguous
- should inspire/stretch/energize

Ownership
- top down does not work
- intent and critical success factors passed down/across organization
- things we have to improve
- areas for breakthrough
- get people's fingerprints on the plan

Line manager
- participant in corporate strategy
- strategist in own right
- provide clarity/direction for unit

Leadership
- strategic thinking skills top priority

1.1 Examine your relationship to the concept of strategy and what makes it work

Answer the following:

1 *Do you have a clear idea of your organization's strategy?*

2 *Do you have a clear idea of how your day-to day activities contribute to achieving that strategy?*

3 *Does the department or work group for which you are responsible have a clearly defined strategic intent?*

4 *Can you articulate it in a sentence?*

5 *Do the people in your work group understand their contribution to your strategic intent?*

6 *Do your people feel a sense of being pulled, stretched, energized, stimulated by the strategic intent?*

7 *What might you have to do to bring your people aboard, i.e. to:*
   (a) enable them to articulate your strategic intent
   (b) understand how it relates to the organization's strategy
   (c) see the context in which their job contributes?

2 Strategy in organizations

About this chapter

This chapter provides a crash course in strategy. It should move the reader from the broad definitions in Chapter 1 to a closer understanding of what strategy looks like in organizations. It will help you develop some versatility in your own strategic thinking and it will show how organizations behave when driven by strategic intent.

Strategy, because it affects and pervades all areas of the business and because, if successful, it brings great rewards, has always aroused considerable interest in business schools. Most postgraduate studies, for example MBAs, devote the greater part of the study time to the subject, and academic credit systems reflect this. The importance afforded to the subject acknowledges, first, that managers will need to be expert at it and, second, that it is a complex and many faceted subject.

To understand better the scope and range of strategy it makes sense to look at the views of some of the main thinkers in the subject. In doing so we will also try to match their views to an example which we can infer from a well-known company. I use the word 'infer' because the strategic plans of prominent organizations are, of course, not public knowledge; on the other hand, the way organizations conduct themselves is reasonably evident and reveals at least aspects of what they are trying to achieve – their strategic intent.

Strategy viewed in terms of the product

Theodore Levitt is the guru in this area and is essentially a marketing person. He is an award-winning Harvard Business School academic and has produced a distinguished body of work (see Bibliography) which, though primarily dealing with concepts of marketing, shed major insight on strategy as well.

 The central tenet of Levitt's work rests on the admirably simple idea that the business of a business is to create and keep customers. All strategy must eventually point to this magnetic north of truth.

A couple of things must, however, be said of this simple definition:

- It is not the *only* duty of the business to create and keep customers; plainly it has a number of other responsibilities which are necessary to sustain it. The business must offer value if it is to keep customers. It must make money if it is to continue to operate, and none of this happens by accident; it must happen by design – i.e. a strategy exists to achieve these things.
- The use of the word 'create' customers is critical. This is not a comment on Levitt's literary style (which incidentally you should sample for its thunderous declamatory nature), it is more an indicator of the imaginative proactivity which is the hallmark of successful businesses. They do not simply meet needs of customers, rather they find the customer and create the need in the first place.

Levitt's total product concept

Levitt has developed a model of a product which has become a standard in both marketing and strategy. It rests on the principle that all products are different from each other and that there is no such thing as a commodity. What makes products different is that surrounding the possibly generic core lies a raft of variables like price, conditions of delivery,

Figure 2.1
A total product concept

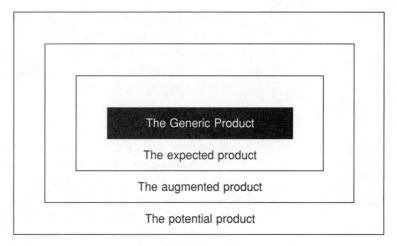

installation, after-sales care etc. These differ depending on how the supplier adjusts these variables so that customers can be created and kept.

The model, a total product concept, as Levitt calls it, looks something like Figure 2.1.

- The *generic product* is the substantive core of what is being offered, say transport in the case of an airline, or the money it can lend in the case of bank.
- The *expected product* represents customers' minimal expectations of that product. The airline must be punctual, safe, have in-flight service etc. The bank must 'look substantial', have known assets etc.
- The *augmented product* goes beyond what the customer expects; the airline serves caviar rather than corned beef on rye, the seats are designed for human beings rather than chimpanzees. The bank actually listens to what you are asking and sells you a service which fits your requirements rather than an approximation on which their margin is high.
- The *potential product* is what might feasibly be offered in the future. This is where the imaginative proactivity of creating customers comes into play. This is the realm of strategist as visionary, a competence to which we must aspire.

It is not hard to see that the boundary between the expected product and the augmented product constantly moves outwards. As a supplier what you might have been able to offer as a unique piece of added value will soon be recognized by your competitors and they too will be offering it. The more competitive the environment in which the product is being transacted, the faster the *expected* fringe will encroach upon the *augmented* product area.

A good example of this is the way banking has moved from a situation where the customer had to show up at the bank during their short opening hours in order to transact business. This led to expanded opening hours, then to twenty-four-hour telephone banking and then to on-demand computer-based home banking. These moves have in part been driven by technology, in part by customer convenience. Not everybody wants twenty-four-hour banking, in fact, not many customers would have articulated this as a need had you asked them. Creating customers is often a matter of shrewd anticipation rather than comprehensive interrogation.

The expansion of *expected* into *augmented* often means that the market becomes fragmented. Not everybody responds positively to the nature of the augmentation. In general, markets become more and more fragmented as more complex and subtly differentiated versions of core products become available. One of the effects of this is that the specific market at which you are aiming becomes more tightly defined, and often more expensive to identify. This leads to a premium value being placed on retaining customers.

A great deal of contemporary strategy addresses the twin objectives of:

- Binding your customers to you so that competitors do not lure them away. Loyalty cards where discounts or benefit points are earned by customers who continue to buy and thus demonstrate their 'loyalty' are becoming more common. In the airline business air miles are a prime means of retaining customers.
- Selling a broader range of products or services to your existing customers, those you can easily reach. Banks cross-selling insurance to borrowers is an excellent example.

Among the best case examples of an organization adopting a strategy which, among other things, moved through Levitt's total product concept model is British Airways.

Operating in a highly competitive and largely undifferentiated field British Airways has consistently worked to improve its product offering since the airline was privatized. A selected history looks like this:

Product augmentation	Intention
Putting People First programme	Designed to improve the interpersonal skills of cabin and ground staff who had previously conducted themselves with a legendary hauteur.
Upgrading of business class to *Club Europe* and *Club World*	Provide a premium business class by strong branding, image, interior design, food, lounges etc.
Aggressive marketing of *World's Favourite Airline*	Advertising, addressed it seems as much to its own staff as to its customers, to establish and maintain clients' perceived differentiation.
Upgrading of First Class – sleeper seats on long hauls	A strong move from expected (and largely undifferentiated) first-class service of other airlines to a credible augmentation of product.

It must be said that over the period the fleet was modernized providing world standard (but undifferentiated) aeroplanes rather than some rather idiosyncratic British-designed aircraft, as had been the case in the past. Air miles are also deployed by

British Airways as a customer-retaining mechanism, though for some strange reason they were introduced many years after US airlines had been offering them.

British Airways may or may not be 'the world's favourite airline' as it claims it is. Nevertheless it was voted by *Fortune* magazine as one of the world's ten most admired companies in 1997.

The operating department and the total product concept

It does not require too great a leap of the imagination to see the application of Levitt's thinking in the context of an operating department within an organization. Each department, unit or team has a product or service output. Each has a group of customers, even if they are internal, within the organization. The expectations of that customer group and the ability of the department to exceed their expectations are key elements in a department's strategy.

Nor is the internal department immune from competition. In these days of outsourcing and of process re-engineering, there is usually an alternative supplier and hence a competitor.

 key concept The key lesson I would like to draw is that the organization or operating unit which can repeatedly redefine and deliver the Potential Product is usually the most successful.

Strategy viewed in terms of markets

Michael Porter, a professor at Harvard Business School, produced during the 1980s a hugely important body of work on strategy (see Bibliography). Porter also provided us with a number of excellent analytical tools some of which we will return to later. Porter's work embraces all aspects of strategy but he is particularly valuable as an example of strategy which is driven by the way an organization should seek to position itself in relation to the markets it serves.

At the heart of Porter's thinking is the concept that corporate strategy seeks to gain and maintain competitive advantage. This is a definition with which one cannot disagree although, as we shall see later, it is a product of a more stable competitive environment than most organizations now experience.

He advised that organizations should dominate specified markets, or segments of specified markets, and make it as hard as possible for others to enter that market. In other words, you get so good at what you are doing that others could not possibly equal or replicate your products and services at the same price and still make money. The heart of the idea is that the cost of entering your markets is so high that potential competitors choose not to try.

Porter's concept of differentiation is broad; successful companies are clearly differentiated from their competitors. Differentiation must, of course, be positive and its nature must also be widely known by the market being served. There is not much sense in being highly differentiated if nobody knows about it.

What this corporate differentiation achieves is that when the customer is in the shopping mode; that is looking for a potential supplier, he or she will match his or her need against known supplier specialities. Getting on to this short list improves your organization's chances of reaping the benefit of the customer's transition from shopping mode to buying mode. Conversely your organization has certain operating cost advantages if, because they know how you are differentiated from others, you attract only well-qualified buyers.

So the ideal is that here we have a well-differentiated organization which serves a defined market segment or segments so well that potential competitors stay away.

Plainly there are not many organizations one can imagine which exactly fit this description, but some get close to it. Usually this degree of market domination implies one of two things: either that the organization is very large, or that it is very specialized.

Let us map a large organization; the British retailer Marks & Spencer (M&S):

Differentiator	Advantage that M&S has developed which is hard for others to replicate
Where it is	Very high traffic sites, large floor space, many sites – for a competitor such sites would no longer be available or only at uneconomic cost.
Value for money	Scale of manufacturing operations – because M&S's suppliers manufacture so many units individual prices can be kept down.
Quality of merchandise	Ability to control manufacturing operations. M&S quality control is legendary and is very hard for others to match at the price.
Product design/ introduction	Knowledge of customers in prime markets. M&S always seems to anticipate fashion correctly – probably they create the fashion.
Product availability	Efficiency of logistical infrastructure. The stock control, warehousing and delivery systems which the company uses assure availability and seem to operate flawlessly.
Inspires customer confidence	Returns policies.
Power of the St Michael brand	The ability to do all of the above consistently.

This map is hardly a comprehensive view of all the things which enable the success of Marks & Spencer. It starts to demonstrate, however, that competitive advantage subsists in getting *everything right that you decide is strategically important*. Getting only some of it right will not give you competitive advantage.

Importantly trying to be better than everyone else at everything is usually a deadly distraction, leads to loss of focus and exhausts your resources.

Just think for a moment what Marks & Spencer chooses not to do particularly well:

- Customer service is OK, not great.
- The product line, though large, is not as comprehensive as that of many smaller retailer groups – choice is limited; it is a one-brand store.
- In-store display is indifferent.
- It does not accept credit cards other than its own.

The internal perspective

As a department within an organization, the concept of 'dominating the market' does not fit very comfortably. The need to do what you do better than any other department within the organization could do it is, however, a necessary strategic commitment.

Most departmental differentiation subsists in functional expertise and in the specific competencies the department has which, usually, do not exist elsewhere in the organization. It is increasingly possible though that similar expertise is accessible from outside the organization.

Dominating a market through the perceived excellence of what you do to serve it must remain a constant strategic aspiration.

The dangers are smugness and myopia, not realizing that ultimately nothing is forever and even the most successful companies are overtaken by determined competitors.

Strategy viewed from a total organization perspective

Ohmae, who holds a Ph.D. in nuclear engineering, dominated strategic thinking and development in Japan from his commanding position as head of McKinsey's Tokyo office. His first book in English, *The Mind of The Strategist*, had a radical effect in the West not least for the use of the word 'mind'. This refocused people on the role of imagination, insight and creativity in the development of strategy, and struck a good balance between the necessary strategic disciplines of information gathering and market analysis on the one hand, and the power of what he called 'inventive élan' on the other.

If Levitt's focus illuminated thinking on product strategy, and Porter's revolved around market dominance, Ohmae gave us the three Cs of the strategic triangle: the corporation, the customers and the competitors.

key concept

Ohmae sees strategy as differentiating yourself from others by providing a stronger matching of corporate capabilities to customer needs. Here the concept of differentiation exceeds simple price and service definitions and extends to all the functional capabilities, characteristics, competencies and skills of the corporation.

Put another way, the strategy should be constructed so that the customer perceives more value being added by more aspects of the organization's activities than is perceived of the competitors.

This concept, though not radically different from either Levitt's or Porter's, adds another facet to strategic thinking by broadening the basis on which strategies must be devised. Nothing which the organization does, no aspect of its activities and relationships with the outside world, should remain unexamined or thought incapable of improvement, enhancement and development.

In many ways Ohmae's thinking is congruent with the Japanese philosophy of continuous improvement which is enshrined in *kaizen*. Here the customer is the bull's-eye of the strategic target. Everything the organization does revolves around adding value in the customer's eyes and thus differentiating the organization.

Adding this value implies an intimate knowledge of the customer's preferences and requirements. Much can be achieved through market analysis, but Ohmae also stresses the need for a detailed observation of customer behaviour.

In thinking about introducing into Japan a range of labour-saving devices for the kitchen, Ohmae observed his wife at work in her own kitchen. He immediately concluded that Japanese kitchen equipment would have to be of smaller physical scale and also provide a more versatile range of applications than American equipment. Storage space is at a premium in Japanese homes so they need small machines capable of many functions.

And another example:

To design the tailgates and boot access to their cars Toyota sent teams into supermarket car parks to observe people shopping. They looked at how people used the storage capacity of the car, what was habitually carried, for how long, how big, how heavy it was and so on. The final designs of sill heights, tailgate access etc. were all affected by the rather obvious but frequently ignored expedient of watching customer behaviour.

Where strategic imagination or 'inventive élan' comes into play is when such observation leads to quite radically different solutions. The Sony Walkman for example could not have been designed by observation of customers or by market analysis. It arose from the imaginative projection of corporate capability, i.e. Sony's skill with radio technology and with electronic miniaturization. These capabilities hatched a radically different product which addressed a vast market that started to behave differently only when the existence of the product enabled it to do so.

The discipline which Ohmae's thinking about strategy provides is that having observed the customer in action, or imagined a mould-breaking alternative product or service, the organization must seek to reverse engineer its abilities to deliver value around every aspect of the product and customer interface. Often the changes this requires in a company are beyond its capacity to sustain and this is why Ohmae uses the word 'match'.

The concept of matching is complex. At its simplest it matches organization capability to customer need. But in determining strategy, with its large future-based component, the matching process implies asking some questions of your organization or department:

- What are we really good at? or At what could we really become good?
- Where do our strengths lie? or Where could we build strengths which differentiate us?

Answering those questions requires an uncomfortable level of honesty on the one hand, and a great deal of firm supporting evidence on the other. The answers must also correspond with a set of customer needs which, when you add your organization's distinctive value, genuinely delivers differentiation and further does so in a future context.

key concept

In the end Ohmae identifies three categories of strategies that emerge from this matching process:

- *Customer-based strategies* – where the primary underlying design of the strategy is to satisfy a clearly designated and segmented customer base as completely as possible.
- *Corporate-based strategies* – where the primary consideration is to apply the organization's specific capabilities, competencies and strengths over a number of customer bases or product lines.
- *Competitor-based strategies* – where the strategy is driven primarily by the need to outperform the competitors to a degree which differentiates your organization. Such strategies often rest on having a lower cost base in your organization, or a better distribution system and so on.

All viable strategies will, of course, have addressed all three of these categories and will overtly deal with them all.

Moving from the theoretical trinity above, let us look at some examples.

British Telecom appears to be following a *customer-based strategy* by offering a product which it is continuously improving while providing the basic service at progressively lower prices. Product enhancements like detailed invoicing, last-call identification, automatic call back and call-waiting services all aim to provide the customer with a more versatile service. At the same time, largely because of deregulation it must be admitted, increasing opportunities for reducing telephone bills are offered; Friends and Family, Premier Line, Country call discounts etc. are all examples of this.

The entry of the major supermarkets into the financial services arena is a fair example of a *corporate-based strategy*. The supermarkets have the huge advantage of large numbers of people walking through their doors and spending time on their premises. Offering these people services which might traditionally be offered by a bank, building society or even a stockbroker is a way of turning this advantage into greater revenue for the store. Because margins on financial products are higher than those with which supermarkets usually deal, this strategy is particularly appealing. It is also causing some misgivings among banks and building societies. Supermarket branding also unlocks a new potential market for financial products; for many the name Sainsbury is more comprehensible and friendly than is the name Barclays Bank.

Dell computers can broadly be said to operate a *competitor-based strategy* in the important area of the personal computer market. Because Dell builds to order rather than supplying from inventory it can afford to supply a customer-specified computer for the same or a lesser price than its competitors.

A moment's reflection on the three examples above will fairly swiftly show that while each strategy described above represents a concentration on one of the three points of Ohmae's triangle of customer, corporation and competitors, the other two points also feature strongly in each.

Total organization strategies in an internal department

Applying Ohmae's thinking to the activities of an internal department helps to provide a context for the appraisal of all aspects of the department's functions and characteristics:

- Is it observing its customers, is it innovating, is it anticipating?
- Is it making the most of its capabilities; the access it has to data or expertise, its experience and so on, to provide a uniquely differentiated service to its customers?
- Is it operating at a price which would be hard for the organization to match elsewhere, inside or outside?

The key lessons which Ohmae provides us with are:

- The concept of 'inventive élan' – bringing creativity, originality, innovation to the strategic process.
- The concept of creating corporate strengths or capabilities and matching them to customer needs, and or competitor differentiation.

What organizational strategy looks like in practice

The strategies of successful organizations are usually built around a core of relatively simple strategic intentions. Over time these intentions spawn a number of tactical initiatives which advance the organization towards its strategic intent on the one hand, and deal with the current operating environment on the other. Figure 2.2 builds on the earlier British Airways example in this chapter, surmises strategic intent (for without insider boardroom knowledge, you cannot know), and interprets some of the visible tactics deployed by British Airways since privatization. The inferences in the figure are not necessarily correct and certainly cannot represent a complete view of British Airways' strategy.

Core strategic intentions			
Enhance the product	Enhance the profits / reduce the costs	Win global share	Attack the competitors
Introduction of *Putting People First* programme to improve interpersonal skills of cabin & ground crew	First tranche of redundancies following privatization		
Upgrading of business class product to *Club World* brand	Focus on more profitable end of the market	Search for off-shore partners Code sharing with other airlines	Acquisition and virtual closure of Caledonian and Dan Air
Aggressive marketing of *World's Favourite Airline* brand	Enhanced IT to predict loading, limit sale of low-priced seats and optimize yield Outsourcing and spin off of non-core activities	Acquisition or partial purchase ... &/or ... licensing of the BA brand ... Deutsche BA TAT (French) US air Quantas and others	Accused of 'dirty tricks' by Virgin
Upgrading of first class – sleeper seats	Start of second major cost reduction leading to strike etc.	Possible alliance with American Airlines	Announces the Go initiative, a new 'no frills' airline

(Left vertical label: **TACTICS**)

Figure 2.2 Strategic intentions: British Airways

Warning

This chapter gives us a broad look at organizational strategy; the views of three of the classical thinkers and a few examples of some major organizational strategies. Work through Activity 2.1 at the end of this chapter and then we move on to the discussions about how the contemporary business environment is changing strategic thinking.

If you stopped reading this book here you would have a very dated and classical idea of what constitutes strategy. The late 1980s and the 1990s have radically changed thinking, and the next two chapters handle this. So read on . . .

Help

↳

Organizational strategy
– create and keep customers
– gain and maintain competitive advantage
– matching organizational capabilities to customer needs

Total product concept
– generic product
– expected product
– augmented product
– potential product

Differentiation
– clearly understood by market segment(s)
– do it better/cheaper than competitors
– dominate the market segment
– competitors cannot afford to enter segment

Strategic triangle – corporation, customers, competitors
– customer centred
– inventive élan/creativity
– matching organizational competence to customer need

2.1 Align yourself with some of the classical thinking about strategy

Think about the following:

Step 1   *Consider the primary product or service your work unit or team provides:*

- *List the qualities or characteristics which are expected of it?*
- *Consider how you might augment the product or service.*
- *If there were no constraints (like cost), what might you be able to make it – the product's or service's potential?*

Step 2   *Think in terms of those who compete with you for the provision of this product or service – remember that if yours is an internal function within the organization it is still possible that others, either inside or outside, might be able to provide what you provide.*

- *List these 'competitors'.*
- *How might you assure that your potential competitors were locked out in the future (i.e. how could you gain and maintain competitive advantage)?*

Step 3   *Assuming you develop a viable scenario or two in Steps 1 and 2, consider:*

- *What particular strengths or capabilities would your work unit need to have in order to support the scenario(s) you have developed?*
- *How might you go about developing these strengths and capabilities?*

STRATEGY IN ORGANIZATIONS

3 Strategy and the changing environment

About this chapter

The contemporary corporate environment is variously described as turbulent, unpredictable, discontinuous (with the past) and in the process of ongoing change. All of this is true and we should take a moment to identify the things which are driving these changes. This is important because, while we cannot change the environment, at least we can target our survival strategies at the drivers of the changes.

In this chapter we are going to look at four main drivers of change:

- *The customer is king* – the rise of a more exacting and discriminating customer and the effect this might have on strategy.
- *Globalization* – how, as the world becomes a single marketplace, competitors become harder to identify and outflank.
- *Technology* – particularly digital technology, and the effect it is having on products and on information.
- *Organizational accountability* – a differing operating environment; organizations having to satisfy more and different stakeholders.

Later we will look at how traditional strategies must need to alter to deal with the different environment these change drivers are creating.

The customer is king

Henry Ford's famous statement that customers could 'have any colour they wanted so long as it is black' could only have been made in a climate in which the availability of the product was exceeded by the demand for it and/or the lack of an alternative. In this climate the power rested in the hands of the manufacturer. Early mass production, if it was to make products at low cost, required that many identical products were made. Cost advantage rested on the scale of manufacture. Customers saw themselves as being well served by the cost advantage and thus easily sublimated any wayward desire for different versions.

Part of the underlying difference between Henry Ford's world in the 1920s and that in the 1990s is the fact that the base rules of manufacture have changed. It is possible to hold costs down as well as to manufacture several different versions of a product.

The compelling underlying difference between our customers and Henry Ford's is that, having experienced progressively increasing opportunities for choice, our customers have come to like it. More, they have come to insist on it, expect the right to exercise it and are even prepared to pay to do so.

At times adaptation to customer choice causes manufacturers to proliferate options beyond the tolerable.

In contrast to Henry Ford's model T, the Fiesta, Ford's best selling car in Europe, is available with 132 different versions of the door trims alone! Multiply this by the range of other options available in the Fiesta, and you compound the potential number of differently specified versions to an astonishing 27 million. Unsurprisingly Ford is moving to cut that number to a mere 10,000 options.

In order to produce products or services which customers will choose above others we have to know a great deal more about the less predictable, less controllable, potentially whimsical nature of customer choice. This is not necessarily easy and the history of product development is littered with examples of misreading customer preference. To use another Ford example, their famous Edsel car is just such a case.

Before building the Edsel, Ford initiated one of the earliest and most far-reaching customer surveys ever undertaken in the motor industry. The aim was to design a car which came as close as possible to being specified by its customers. The Edsel, when it was rolled out, proved ugly even by the design standards of the time and, ultimately, the car provided Ford with an expensive flop.

But further to compound the problem there is a history of extremely successful products which, had you asked the customer in the first place, would never have been developed. It is hard to imagine customers specifying 3M's amazingly successful Post-it notes for example.

However, devising the right products is just part of the problem because to achieve satisfied customers, those who will continue to buy your products or services, they must be served with a far more complex set of requirements. In her book *Kaizen Strategies for Customer Care,* Pat Wellington devotes twenty-six pages of definition to the elements of and standards for customer care. It is well worth reading.

In-company supplier/customer relationships

Within an organization each of the operating departments can usually be looked upon as a process in the value chain. Each is likely to be flanked on one side by suppliers and on the other by customers. The invariable tendency is to increase the specification on the supplier side of the relationship while at the same time decreasing it on the customer side. Most line managers will be familiar with this unsurprising phenomenon because they invariably wear both supplier and customer hats.

As time goes on functional units can become extremely good at what they are doing; the process they are executing or the value they add in the chain. These could become 'organizational chimneys' – they continuously hone their expertise in the context of how they believe it be improved. They become hungry for resources and they become cut off from customer need.

It is to redress this tendency that many organizations resort to outsourcing, cross-functional teaming, business process re-engineering etc. – all those techniques which force upon the organization the disciplines of competing for customers. In fact, the discipline of competition has become one of the main ways in which companies achieve reorganization, shed cost and improve productivity.

More, the whole process of deregulation has at its heart the need to compete for this increasingly demanding and fickle customer.

At no time previously has the customer exercised such power over the supplier. Strategies which do not put the customer centre stage are doomed to failure.

Additionally customers are less predictable, less loyal and apparently more whimsical than ever before. He or she is a moving target of ever changing needs, perceptions, beliefs, experiences, fashions and lifestyle changes; keeping up with him or her is, of itself, a strategy.

Competition for the customer is one of the primary productivity improvement techniques being deployed inside organizations, between organizations, by governments and even by supra-national entities like the European Union (EU).

Globalization

Globalization is best described by the 'global village' concept. Wherever you live, your day-to-day life is increasingly affected by products, services, practices, customs, belief systems, investments, information and so on from countries and cultures other than your own. Though these cultures are spatially remote from where you are, access to some of their attributes is as easy as if they were in the same village. Communication and transportation around the world is fast and, compared with the past, relatively inexpensive. This means that to all intents and purposes, much of the world is on your doorstep.

In terms of day-to-day competitive strategy, it may have been possible twenty years ago to know and evaluate your competitors because they were, figuratively speaking, just up the street. Now, however, your competitive position in London may be changed by decisions taken in Seoul to invest in Milan. Because Italy and Britain are part of a common market, lo and behold, you have another UK competitor. Your customers now also have the ability to make purchases almost anywhere in the world with their credit cards, or by their access to information which you may not have. Even knowing or anticipating who your competitors are can be a problem, let alone competing with them.

Easy transportation and information also enables organizations to source various activities in countries where the job can be better or less expensively done (even counting the shipping costs) than it can in the organization's prime markets. Doing this can provide a cost saving, and hence a competitive advantage. Currency conversion rates and their fluctuation are also constantly affecting strategic sourcing decisions.

- Hewlett Packard will solve problems you may have with their computers from California, India or the UK depending on which of their service centres is on-line when you have the problem.
- Your Ford will contain components made in half a dozen different countries and a dozen different factories.
- If you live in the UK each of the eight ingredients of your Chinese stir fry can easily have been imported from a different country – none of them China.

With the fall of the Berlin wall the scope of globalization has been hugely extended because the economic and information constraint exercised by Communist political regimes has vanished. Arguably even more importantly, the liberalization of the Chinese and Indian economies massively enhances the population base which participates in feeding the complexities of globalization.

The effects of globalization are likely to intensify as tariffs and trade barriers are increasingly eroded. This will compound the unpredictability of the competitive environment on the one hand though it offers more opportunities for strategic diversity on the other hand.

Strategic thinking has to fit into this unfamiliar environment to take advantage of the opportunities it offers while also being aware of the risks globalization poses.

Digital technology

In 1947 at Bell Laboratories in New Jersey the first transistor was demonstrated. Essentially this is a device which amplifies an electric current and switches it on or off. It is on this base that the 'digital revolution' is founded, for the simple properties of a transistor are fundamental to the storage, retrieval and transmission of information. Link a number of transistors together and you have a microchip. An Intel Pentium II chip can do 588 million calculations per second and so you have a prodigious, unimaginably huge, capability to store, retrieve and move information. Add to this two facts:

- Microprocessor capability doubles in capacity and halves in relative cost every eighteen months – Moore's law.
- Intel, the world's largest chip manufacturer, persistently and with huge success expands the range of uses and applications of chips; during 1996 3.6 billion microprocessors were sold embedded – i.e. for specific applications like monitoring the fuel injection in your car, programming your washing machine or controlling

your air-conditioning system. We read that even the classic Lego brick which has provided low-technology entertainment for generations of children is in the future to have a microchip embedded in it.

From this welter of extravagant figures, it is easy to see that the effect of digital technology on almost every aspect of our lives will accelerate exponentially in the future.

It really is quite hard to imagine what all this implies in terms of strategic planning, but a few 'so whats?' do come clearly through:

Technology will *revolutionize the nature of existing products*, making them more sophisticated, more versatile, probably more durable. The strategic implication of this is that product design will make more innovative use of technology, product life cycles will continue to shorten, product 'versioning' will proliferate, product ranges will broaden, and more, previously unthought of, products will appear.

More 'so whats?':

Access to information of high quality, swift retrievability and recent currency will be available – and it will be available to all. The strategic implication is that competitive advantage will not be delivered by having access to unique information but rather *how you use or interpret the information will help to differentiate*.

The *channels by which we reach our markets will change* because customers will have a wider variety of sources of product information and supply. The Internet, in particular, will affect shopping patterns as with globalization above. The strategic implications here are that entry costs to markets may well fall, niche markets may be more easily reached, but also that all markets will be harder to defend.

Technology will affect the *way in which products are made and services provided.* Production line 'truths' will continue to be redefined; fewer people will be used, greater flexibility becomes possible. In strategic terms the base financial equations of manufacturing costs, adding of value and where margin or profit is taken will change.

Other technologies

While digital technology, affecting as it does information and communication, is an obvious driver of our changing environment, it is reasonable to assume that the full panoply of technological advances will have an impact on organizational strategy. In particular biotechnology, since it will radically affect the food chain, health, demographics and lifestyles, is not only an industry itself, but a driver of underlying change which will create new markets and new product possibilities. Nanotechnology, too, building devices on a molecular scale and manipulating material atom by atom, must also greatly affect our future.

Since strategic thinking must entertain a future perspective, the serious consideration of the medium-term effects of technology on the organization, its customers, its markets and the products and services it offers is an essential discipline of strategy development.

This is no less true for strategy development of a department within an organization than it is for any customer directed business.

Organizational accountability

Asked to reflect on the company of the future, Britain's Royal Society of Arts developed a concept which they called the 'licence to operate'. Graphically this looks like Figure 3.1.

Figure 3.1
The 'licence to operate'
concept

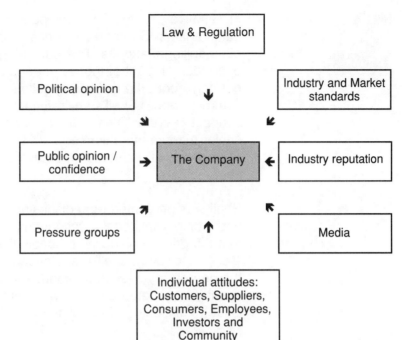

The organization is surrounded by a number of interest groups whose collective approval of, and confidence in, how the organization is conducting itself either allows or obstructs its operations. Some of these interest groups have always been there, law and regulation for example. But two things are happening:

- 'Traditional' interest groups become more intrusive into company operations – regulators, industry watchdogs, Health and Safety authorities etc.; all are exercising increasing levels of influence.
- More interest groups are emerging, and the company has to be sensitive in recognizing them and satisfying their agendas.

When an organization is, for example, defending itself against media attack or justifying itself in the eyes of an environmental lobby, its energies are seriously deflected from focusing on its customers and competitors.

In 1997 we saw the Shell company fighting and losing a battle against Greenpeace concerning the disposal of one of its drilling platforms. This particular battle cost Shell an enormous amount of money. It generated press coverage not only about the issue in question, but also critical comment about Shell's environmental and political conduct in West Africa. Such a battle takes up valuable senior management time and it also affects the perceptions of the company's customers, suppliers and shareholders.

Shell was prevented from disposing of the platform as it had intended although subsequently Greenpeace agreed that the original plan was probably the most acceptable. More importantly Shell's reputation probably suffered from the degree of adverse comment and critical reportage the event had generated which was quite tangential to the issue of disposing of the platform.

Viewed another way, the diversity of interests represented by the 'licence to operate' can be employed as components of organizational differentiation. Body Shop, for example, differentiates itself very successfully as 'eco-friendly' and by its public commitments not to test its products on animals. It is hard to know what such a differentiation is worth in terms of attracting and retaining customers; what we do know is that maintaining the differentiation radically affects the behaviour of the company in that it must constantly demonstrate to its client base and to a watchful external world that it is behaving in accordance with its declared values.

The use of the word 'watchful' above is important because the interest groups whose collective 'permission' helps lubricate an organization's operations are not necessarily discrete groups. Increasingly the employees of organizations are also its shareholders, and often its customers as well. Add to this the fact that many of these people have ethical beliefs and values which they wish the organization to espouse. The organization has then to pitch its strategy, and hence its day-to-day behaviour, in a way which illuminates its commitments to the different interests represented. The latitude for organizational hypocrisy in the sense of dysfunction between what it says and the way it actually behaves is, happily, narrow and decreasing.

There is a great deal of evidence to suggest that those organizations which succeed in managing the multiplicity of relationships inherent in the 'licence to operate' model are a great deal more successful.

This thinking underpins the conditions of the prestigious US Baldridge Award (see also Chapter 15, 'Aspiring to excellence', in this book). The award is not, as often thought, simply a quality award in the traditional product/service/satisfied customer sense, but a quality award judged in the context of all the key relationships of the organization. Incidentally, companies which have achieved the Baldridge Award show above average financial returns as well. In the UK the Business Excellence Model developed by the British Quality Foundation addresses the same broad spectrum of relationships and seeks to achieve excellence in each.

The point of importance here is that the strategy of the organization has to be viewed through many more lenses than simply those of the customer and the competition.

On the positive side this provides more opportunities for differentiation.

On the negative side it means that strategy development becomes more complex and has to address constituencies and interest groups which may not advance the organization's success but could frustrate its ability to perform.

Help

Changed operating environment

Customer is king
– customer choice proliferating; versioning
– markets are fragmenting; smaller niches
– know your customer/beware of pitfalls of
  customers specifying

Globalization
– harder to predict who your competitors are
– opportunities for strategic diversity, e.g.
  manufacturing elsewhere

Digital technology
– the ubiquitous chip
– more chips in more products
– implications for product design and . . .
– product life cycle
– use of information more important because
  everyone has access
– channels to markets change
– affect how products are made

Other technologies
– watch biotechnology/nanotechnology

*Strategy is future focused, hence reading technology
right is key*

Organizational accountability
– licence to operate
– multiple stakeholders to be satisfied
– further opportunities for differentiation
– 'excellence' subsists in managing all stakeholder
  relationships

Your operating environment

This activity helps you to map out the operating environment of your organization or work unit so that you have done some thinking about it when we move into the process of developing strategy.

Step 1 *Write down three ways in which your customers' needs have changed in the last year.*
Consider three ways in which customers' needs will change in the next year.
Speculate on the basic characteristics of your customers' needs in three years' time.

Step 2 *Write down the names of your current top three competitors.*
Consider whether they will be there in three years' time.
Consider who else may be there in three years' time.

Step 3 *Consider three ways in which technology will change the product or service you offer in the next year.*
Consider three ways in which technology will change the way in which you manufacture or deliver your product or service.

Step 4 *List the pending laws, regulations (national, supra-national – e.g. EU – or industry based) which are likely to affect your organization or work unit within the next year.*
List the pressure groups or lobbies which might affect your organization or work unit.

Step 5 *Look at what you have written down and ask yourself:*

- *How sure am I of what I have written down?*
- *Which areas do I feel pretty certain about?*
- *Which areas do I feel pretty uncertain about?*
- *How might I gather the information I need to map the future?*

4 The breakdown of traditional strategies

The story so far

So far we have established two things:

- a shared understanding of what organizational strategy is
- a brief review of those things which are driving change in the operating environment of all organizations.

If you need a review, look back at the help screens at the end of each chapter. It is important that we carry through this thinking and try to paint a picture of how the nature of strategy defined in Chapters 1 and 2 is changing because of the environmental changes described in Chapter 3.

This short chapter shows how traditional strategies break down in a world which is in a state of rapid and discontinuous change. If we understand how it is that things go wrong, we will be better able to focus on viable strategies for our own organizations.

In the meantime it is cautionary to consider some facts produced by Shell on the durability of the market leaders. Surveying *Fortune* magazine's top 500 companies which existed in 1970, Shell found that by 1983, one-third of them had ceased to exist. Size and success is no guarantee of longevity; the length of your corporate life is more directly related to the quality of your strategy than it is to your corporate strength.

Why strategies fail

To see why strategies fail let us look at a simplified representation of classic supplier/marketing positioning across the market for a product. To make the model work we have to assume that the product we are talking of is available in a wide range of differentiated options. A range of washing machines might be an example with, at the one end, a standard no frills automatic, at the other a high technology, silent, multiple cycle, eco-friendly machine.

The market and its suppliers might be represented along a continuum as shown in Figure 4.1.

Figure 4.1

Market Segments i.e. Groups of self-selecting customers

Market Segments i.e. Groups of self-selecting customers

Suppliers of **Low Price Lower 'Quality'** Product

Suppliers of **High Price Higher 'Quality'** Product

The strategy pursued by each of the suppliers in this classic case is:

- Each operates within its defined segment addressing its promotion to the media familiar to the segment; distributing through channels frequented by the segment, and producing incremental product or service improvements which add value when viewed through the quality lens of the segment.
- As far as possible, through their ability to do the above better than anyone else, they are able to defend their dominant position in the segment.
- To compete for growth, each supplier erodes the edges of the market segments adjacent to it.

But, because of

- the customer being king, all customers now want high quality at low cost; and because of
- globalization, others are entering the markets who do not respect this orderly arrangement; and also because of
- globalization, they can make cheaper products in Korea at the same quality specification; and because of
- technology, the product now has, say, built in microchips which radically redefines its 'quality' parameters.

The entry of this new player into the market forces each of the traditional suppliers into a defensive mode – usually the weaker strategic position. Under these circumstances organizations will quite mistakenly and myopically declare their product to be of better quality when it manifestly is not. They will claim that customers will be loyal to the brand which also usually turns out to be a naive piece of self-delusion.

Resources are often committed to try to preserve a market position which is *de facto* untenable. Organizations will savagely erode their margins to compete on price when price is no longer the primary battlefield. They will commit selling and marketing resources in profligate sums to restore a market position which cannot be regained by selling and marketing means. Finally, they will accept the newly defined parameters and either play by them or resign the field.

Now it would be tempting to look at the scenario above and label it unusual, unrealistic or unjustifiably gloomy. The fact is that it is none of these things. The theoretical situation described is common, it happens constantly, and even the most powerful organizations are not immune to its effects.

---

key concept

Traditional strategies depending on dominating given markets now rarely work for a prolonged period.

Market leadership once gained by an organization is usually lost to a more innovative or agile competitor and, usually, only regained by similar exercise of innovation and agility.

THE BREAKDOWN OF TRADITIONAL STRATEGIES

It is true that most of the time competing organizations are in a steady state of catch-up. An innovation introduced by A is rapidly copied by B, improved on by C, and so on. This means that the status quo is only temporarily disrupted with organizations leapfrogging each other as a floating proportion of market moves between a defined group of suppliers.

Essentially the length of time this situation can persist is limited; two things constrain its continuance:

- Competing in this way rarely provides the financial margins, the revenue growth and hence the profitability for the organization to thrive.
- If the intrinsic growth of the market is large enough, such is the ferocity of the contemporary competitive climate that a deep-pocketed competitor is likely to move in and redefine the game.

What do we mean by 'redefine'?

A market is redefined when the primary basis for the purchasing decision changes. In the washing machine model above we have assumed that the technological superiority of the machine with the microchip is such that people want no other, even at the slightly reduced price of the technologically inferior models.

Let us look at some real examples.

The mighty US car industry, dominated by what were at the time the largest and most profitable companies in the history of time, General Motors and Ford, failed to see a market redefinition when customers demonstrated they valued fuel economy over size and styling.

This failure enabled Japanese manufacturers to gain significant market share in the domestic strongholds of the US giants, a situation which was hardly imaginable until it happened. It took some years for US manufacturers to catch up.

Then it happened again; Japanese cars, by providing a significantly better level of quality and reliability than their American competitors, led the US customer to redefine the market by requiring these levels of quality and reliability as a precondition for purchase. Again the Japanese manufacturers gained share and the US giants were forced into catch-up mode.

IBM dominated the computing market for more than a generation and became the most profitable firm in the world in the process. Its dominant market position arose from its huge installed base of mainframe computers.

The rise of the personal computer (PC) must have seemed to IBM not to be a redefinition of the market, for while IBM entered the field it did so more than two years after the redefinition occurred – it missed the wave. It then failed to mobilize the organizational commitment to attack the market with the energy and zeal needed.

Perhaps it was organizational hubris which prevented IBM from joining the competitive slugging match which was needed in the redefined market. Perhaps it was the need to protect its installed mainframe base, or perhaps IBM had had it their own way for so long that it had forgotten the realities of tough competition. In any event the company suffered near fatal losses but returned from the brink smaller, less influential and, hopefully, wiser.

The IBM example above introduces another characteristic of market behaviour. In one sense the emergence of the PC was a market redefinition in that money which might previously have been spent on mainframes was now spent on PCs. In another sense, however, the original market still continued. IBM's mainframe base remains its bread and butter.

The redefinition of the information technology (IT) market might then more accurately be described as a market split – in this case the offspring representing a far larger potential than the original.

THE BREAKDOWN OF TRADITIONAL STRATEGIES

It is salutary, too, to take a look at the redefinition of the employment market, particularly the employment market for managers.

Management hierarchies developed so that the will of the top people within the organization could be executed. Messages were passed down through layers of intermediary relays at each of which they were interpreted and recommunicated. Compliance was assured and control was exercised by this hierarchy as well.

This model has persisted from the start of industrial revolution, and probably owes its existence to earlier models for controlling large complex organizations like government, armies etc.

Communication technology, the need for cost reduction, different working and employment ethics have all rendered this system obsolete. It is hard to estimate the employment mortality rate of the middle managers who would have been needed to sustain the hierarchical model but two sets of numbers are indicative.

In the 1970s the estimate for the loss of white-collar jobs in the USA stood at 2.5 million. In Britain the proportion of 50+-year-old males not working nor looking for work had risen from 7 per cent in 1975 to 28 per cent by 1997 – these are the people who would most probably have constituted the components or nodes of this management system.

Today the organization, as customer, is buying different skills from those it bought in the days of hierarchy. It behoves those who wish to continue to be employed by organizations to have a strategy for adding value in the eyes of this increasingly demanding customer.

It is also imperative that the department or team for which each middle manager is responsible should equally regard its continued existence as conditional upon its ability to satisfy its organizational customer(s).

What emerges from this is that it becomes a strategic imperative that the supplier anticipates, or more profitably initiates, the redefinition of the market.

None of the above vitiates the strategic truths of Chapter 2. Organizations should still be seeking to make 'potential' rather than 'expected' products, to seek to dominate their chosen sectors of markets and to match their capabilities to their customers' perception of value.

What has changed the game is that the environment in which organizations seek to deploy their strategy is less stable, less predictable and less continuous with the past.

Put simply:

- things change, requiring strategies which are flexible or directional rather than prescriptive; and because
- things change faster, strategies must anticipate a wide range of tactical responses which must happen fast; and because
- things change more radically, strategies must be in a constant state of review, reappraisal or fine tuning.

This leads us, in Chapter 5, to start to lay out the components of successful modern strategies and then, in Chapter 6, to the process of developing your own strategy.

4.1 A reflection

It has become a truism to say that things are changing fast, but the reality is that as we live through it, we often fail to assess just how radically and quickly things do change.

Step 1   *Think of a piece of capital equipment you or your company may own – select something which replaced an earlier version and which may, in the next year or two, be itself replaced.*

Step 2   *List the suppliers who might have tendered to provide the existing piece of equipment.*
List the suppliers who might have tendered to provide the predecessor piece of equipment.
List the suppliers who might tender for the replacement piece of equipment.

Step 3   *For each of the three pieces in the series; predecessor, existing and potential replacement, list:*

- *The actual or probable buying criteria.*
- *The actual or probable price compared to a standard like your own salary.*
- *The actual or probable other conditions of sale the successful supplier might have or will offer.*

Step 4   *What conclusions do you draw from the competitive environment previous, current and future for the piece of equipment?*

Note: Frequently this exercise proves impossible because the item selected will never be replaced since its function has been superseded by an entirely different means of providing the outcome for which it was originally manufactured. Such a result makes its own compelling statement of the rate and nature of change.

5 What makes successful modern strategies?

So we have a fairly apocalyptic view of the effects of change on traditional strategy and it now makes sense to look at the things which help us devise a strategy which is likely to survive in discontinuous and turbulent times.

In dealing with this, I would like to go back to the simple four-part concept we developed in Chapter 1, and expand it in terms of the characteristics of successful contemporary strategy.

First, let us turn the model around:

- *Strategic purpose* – what, as an organization, we are here to do.
- *Strategic intent* – where we will concentrate our energies so that we can deliver our purpose long term.
- *Critical success factors* – what has to go right for us to achieve our strategic intent.
- *Core competencies* – what strengths we will have to develop to manage the organization so that we can achieve our strategic intent.

Next, let us look at each of these in turn.

Strategic purpose

There was a time, not very long ago, when, if you put the question 'What is the purpose of this business?' to a group of its managers, the unanimous, spontaneous and almost reflexive answer would be: 'To make money.'

It used to be a knock-down, drag-out fight to demonstrate that making money was not the purpose of the business, merely a precondition for its continuity. Without wanting to labour the point unduly, the 'make money' answer is like defining the purpose of a motor car as 'to burn fuel'. The car will not function without fuel, the business will not function without money. Neither the vehicle nor the organization was conceived for that purpose however.

True, in not-for-profit organizations more purpose-directed answers did and do emerge. As time has gone on the multiple responsibilities of the organization are increasingly recognized by more people. The same question about purpose starts to generate a list which does not look too different from the model of organizational accountability we developed in Chapter 3 (see Figure 3.1).

The downside of this kind of detailed response is that it errs on the side of overcomplication and also tends to obscure the underlying purpose of the organization.

The purpose of an organization, whether a business or a not-for-profit organization, is best described as providing a defined outcome to a defined category of users or customers.

Note the use of the word 'outcome' – i.e. your purpose is not the provision of a product or a service; your purpose is something the current product or service currently achieves for your customers.

The purpose of . . .	is not to . . .	but rather to . . .
Butterworth-Heinemann, the publishers of this book	publish books	educate and entertain.
The Benefits Agency	pay money to the disadvantaged	ease hardship and maintain minimum living standards.
The Prudential	sell insurance	provide a safety net to mitigate the effects of mishap.

If this looks like hair-splitting, be cautioned to take it with the utmost seriousness. One of the greatest strategic pitfalls is to focus too much on the current product or service of the organization. This sort of focus leads to incremental improvement of what is available now and virtually precludes the possibility of the organization redefining a market.

History is littered with examples of organizations so fixated on the existing product or service they supplied that when the purpose of the product was delivered by new and different means, they frequently missed the opportunity of capitalizing on the infrastructure they had created.

- Shipping companies failed to become major airlines.
- Traditional fabric manufacturers lost the provision of synthetic textiles to the chemical companies.
- Film-makers by and large failed to exploit the opportunities of television broadcasting.
- Newspapers and magazine publishers failed to become the providers of news to the broadcasters.

But here is a good positive example.

There is a story the truth or accuracy of which I have never been able to verify, but it provides a handy example. It concerns Procter and Gamble who sought to limit the environmental damage of using phosphates in the provision of detergents.

As long as the company saw itself as a major supplier of a range of detergent products it grappled with the problem of inventing a phosphate-free detergent. If it saw its role as providing the means for its customers' cleanliness, however, it could redefine the framework of its problem-solving.

The story goes that it is that redefinition which led to the invention of Pampers, the disposable nappies. Rather than launder dirty nappies with detergents, the customer could throw the dirty ones away and achieve the cleanliness purpose.

Later in the book when we look at actually developing a strategy of your own, we will look at some questions which should help you to determine purpose. In the meantime accept that the organizations which are really clear about the benefits they provide to their customers are those with the best long-term prognosis.

Strategic intent

The second major component of successful strategies is establishing and clarifying the organization's strategic intent. In reality this exercise usually generates a number of related statements, each usually a strategic *intention* which collectively serve to describe the organization's overall strategic intent.

We spoke about strategic intent in Chapter 1 and gave a few examples. In the more complex and less predictable world in which we now operate, being clear about it tends to be a bit harder. What makes it difficult is that organizations must make a number of guesses at what the future is going to be like in order that they can position themselves in that future environment and then express that positioning as strategic intent.

Many organizations confront this problem by trying to understand the following questions:

- What industry are we playing in?
- What does the future of that industry look like?
- Where can we add unique or special value?
- What are the financial implications and expectations of the industry we operate in and the area in which we will add value?

Useful as it would be if this catechism provided a logical chain, most organizations find that it does not. The questions are mutually interdependent and whatever order they are handled in the import of the answers constantly leads the strategist to backtrack and reconsider. If the organization is well able to describe the future of the industry and markets in which it will be operating, then it is more likely to be able to define a viable strategic future for itself. It is also able to underpin that future with the financial return necessary to sustain it and to satisfy its owners.

If, on the other hand, the organization is simply reactive to events unaware of, or unthinking about, the consequences of what is driving the industry, it is unlikely that it can define a strategic intent. It is also unlikely that it will survive for long in the competitive turbulence it will encounter.

Determining the industry in which the organization is operating may seem to be blindingly self-evident but traditional industry divisions are constantly blurring; industries which historically have been thought of as separate are merging and new opportunities are emerging all the time.

The computer industry, for example, is about designing and manufacturing hardware. It is about developing software, it is about telecommunications, it is about entertainment, it is about education. It is daunting for an organization to commit to a longer term strategic intent when today's market definitions are already difficult to determine while the future looks even less clear. If an organization is in any of the segments of this increasingly homogeneous industry, it might be tempted to ask itself whether it should not be in another part as well.

This leads, for example, to software houses wondering whether they should not be in the entertainment business, or hardware manufacturers wondering whether they should be software providers (see IBM's purchase of Lotus for example) and so on. Obtaining a clear and realistic view not only of the opportunities the industry may provide, but also of the viability and potential for your own organization in a given segment, requires incisive, informed and very thorough thinking.

Hard as it is to establish strategic intent, it is made easier when the organization has a clear idea of its *purpose*. Purpose will not define strategic intent, but it will create a clear idea of the arenas in which the organization will be playing.

It is usually as important for the organization to decide what it will not do in the future as it is for it to decide what it will do.

Of course there are industries which are much more orderly, where evolution is slower and potentially more predictable. Finding space in such an industry is inherently more simple but it is fraught with the danger of succumbing to the narcotic effect of complacency – see the IBM example in Chapter 4. It is not for nothing that Andy Grove, Chairman of Intel, called his 1997 book *Only the Paranoid Survive.*

Serious strategic planners have to engage in a kind of iterative process which consistently assesses potential intention against the change-drivers identified in Chapter 3, i.e. customers, the effects of globalization and competition, the effect of technology and, finally, the effect of broader organizational accountability.

Achieving clarity of intent around strategy then sets up the strategist to guess where the money will be made in the environment identified. Traditional concepts of margin, processes for adding value, even definitions of value, are probably changing and the longer-term view of this can also affect the strategic intention.

examples

It has been an object of faith in the car industry for years that the real money is not made from the sale of the new car, but rather from the ongoing parts and service revenue the sale initiates.

A common strategy then has been for manufacturers and dealerships to discount initial purchase prices in order to secure the resulting, higher-margin service revenue.

In a changing world where customer requirements insist that service intervals lengthen, and for fewer parts and systems failures, the potential for post-sale, high-margin revenue is becoming constrained.

This leads dealerships and manufacturers to give serious thought as to where in the supply chain of motor vehicles the most profitable opportunities might lie in the future.

The strategic intent of an organization always addresses a financial objective as one of its component intentions. How this is defined varies enormously and might be expressed as: profit, return on investment, a desired rate of volume growth, market share etc. When an in-house department or team is developing a strategy, financial considerations will also always surface. The umbrella organization under which the department or function operates is, of itself, a buyer of the department's services and will thus, just as any other customer, have very clear ideas of the value of that service to the organization.

If we look back at the British Airways examples we inferred where we offered four statements of strategic intent we can see that a relatively simple one-line statement is often enough. Enough that is to mark out or delineate a whole area of corporate strategic thinking and planning the intent of which is understood throughout the organization. 'Being a global airline', for example, is a shorthand heading under which a huge amount of corporate effort is mobilized. Each of the statements of strategic intent similarly compels the attention and the activity of the airline to achieve it.

Strategic intent is a mutually understood series of statements of the organization's longer-term intentions. It helps describe the position of the organization in the future and should:

- clearly define the major areas in which organizational energy will be channelled
- deal with how the organization intends to compete
- address a considered financial expectation or aspiration
- help the employees of the organization to build viable operational objectives to achieve all aspects of the intent
- be a source of aspiration sufficient to capture the discretionary effort of employees
- be seen as worthwhile, ethical, involving and rewarding
- above all it must be shared with and be understood by everybody.

Vision

Given that modern strategic intent is less precise than its now defunct predecessor, the strategic plan, most organizations find it valuable to spend time developing a vision – how and what we would like the organization to be in the future. Creating an agreed set of qualitative descriptions about the way the organization will look and feel in the future usually turns out to be an interesting, enjoyable and inspiring exercise. Employees enjoy participation, they are interested in hearing the vision of their peers and their bosses, and they are usually keen to contribute.

The strategic vision is in a way a destination which we are trying to reach. But like all visions, there is a shared understanding that we will never reach it but rather that it provides a point of orientation, and a point of aspiration. It can be a star to steer towards.

Values

The values express the rules of the game; what is allowed and what is not allowed. Such values help define the ethics of the organization and help describe how it will align itself with its internal and external responsibilities.

A clearly understood series of statements of strategic intent supported by a shared vision and an agreed set of organizational values provide a set of control systems, parameters or points of reference in which individuals in the organization, at all levels, can operate with confidence and consistence.

There was a time when the old mission statement emerged cut and dried from on high to the mild surprise of all employees who filed and forgot it. Now we find organizations putting a high degree of effort into collectively establishing purpose, collectively establishing strategic intent, collectively establishing vision and collectively establishing values. Doing it this way enables employees to align themselves with the strategy and to influence its formulation from their uniquely valuable coal-face experience of the organization's processes.

My experience is that when organizations really seek to involve employees in all aspects of the development of strategic intent there is a dramatic improvement in the potential likelihood of it being achieved. Further, through mutually agreed and established parameters of vision and values, the organization also achieves its intent in the way it wants to.

In their fascinating book *Competing for the Future*, Hamel and Pralahad describe the process by which Electronic Data Systems (EDS) involved its managers internationally in the development of its new strategy.

Starting in 1992, and working from an enormously successful market and profit position, EDS sought to revitalize its strategy and compete more aggressively for the future.

Taking over a year, it involved over 2,000 people operating in a series of 'waves' – groups of managers working on specified areas for discovery. Apparently 30,000 workhours were devoted to the project, much of it in private time and much of it involving extreme personal effort.

In truth the exercise at EDS had a scope larger than establishing strategic intent, but the lesson here is in the degree of involvement and the commitment to a shared view of the future.

Later, when we deal with the processes for building strategy, we will return to the means by which we can build strategic intent.

Once we have clarity about strategic purpose, i.e. what we are here to do, and have thought through our strategic intent, i.e. where will we concentrate our energies so that we can deliver our purpose long term, we have to start thinking about implementation. This immediately leads us to the next stage, critical success factors.

Critical success factors

Determining critical success factors requires that we move from the future directed view necessary to determine long-term purpose and long-term strategic intent, and focus on the implications of achieving the aspiration we have set for ourselves. It implies examining the distance between the aspiration and the current condition, and determining some of the 'whats' which will have to be achieved, as distinct from the 'hows' which are the ways in which we achieve them.

Here is an example, inferred from consultancy work undertaken by the author with the Bank of Ireland, developing its strategy in the period immediately after financial deregulation.

Strategic intention	Critical success factors – what had to go right
To become a provider of a broader base of financial services	To develop a range of new financial products To cross-sell, i.e. new financial products to the bank's existing client base
To reduce operating costs	To create a category of employees who were not subject to existing 'expensive' union agreements To create a computer system capable of centralizing and hence cutting the cost of 'back office' work
To seek growth opportunities offshore	Identify and acquire a US bank Identify and acquire appropriate English financial services providers

Note: These examples in no way encapsulate the whole of the Bank of Ireland's strategic plan, and also do not document each of the strategic intentions it had set itself.

As you can see from this example, establishing the critical success factors starts to provide a set of macro-objectives which, it might be argued, for the first time bring the process of strategy development into a planning mode. For those who are new to the strategy development exercise, suddenly the light starts to dawn and the processes of developing purpose, strategic intent (vision and values), which were probably seen as worthy but time-wasting, achieve relevance as the critical success factors fall out.

The average line manager is now on home territory and can rapidly start to translate the critical success factors (CSFs) into action plans, set objectives for employees, prepare resource allocations, set up critical paths and so on. In other words what is happening is that we are moving from the 'whats', the CSFs, towards the 'hows', the action plan.

Realize too that CSFs change as time goes on. While strategic intent is likely, if we have developed it properly, to point a consistent general direction over time, CSFs will define things which we have to fix or get right now. Once we have got one CSF right, another is likely to surface to replace it.

Critical success factors should really mobilize the concentration of the organization and should be recognized for what they are – that is *critical* to the *success* of the strategy. For this reason endowing nice-to but not need-to objectives with the CSF label is likely to devalue the CSF and it is likely to diffuse the energy of the organization into too many areas.

The hard questions of criticality must be confronted: 'What will happen if we don't achieve this?' If the answer is 'nothing much' then you have not got a CSF. If the answer is that we would have to go another route to support the strategic intent, then you probably have got a CSF.

While the examples cited above are pretty hard edged and easy to understand, CSFs are not always as tangible. The fact that a CSF may be a bit difficult to quantify does not necessarily compromise its criticality. Sometimes, when a CSF emerges, nobody is sure how to measure whether it is achieved or not. The following Marriott Hotels example demonstrates this.

Marriott Hotels International, confronting a market in which there was an oversupply of hotel rooms in the late 1980s, embarked on a strategy which would seek to differentiate the chain from others by the degree of customer satisfaction it would achieve.

Marriott had and has a good reputation for the quality of its accommodation, the way in which its premises are maintained and the physical attributes of its hotels. To improve customers' satisfaction it realized that the interaction of select staff (front office, concierges and contact staff) with the customers was critical.

A combination of training and empowerment was embarked upon to achieve this. The empowerment element sought to provide employees ('associates' as Marriott calls them) with defined discretion for problem-solving. This meant that under given circumstances an associate could correct an error, make amends to the customer without seeking higher permission, sign-offs etc.

Implementation of the programme was initially greeted as 'flavour of the day' by Marriott associates. It became imperative that the senior management of the organization demonstrate by their commitment and by their behaviour that the initiative was critical to Marriott's strategy. The 'needle' of customer satisfaction only started to move when this top-down commitment started to change the Marriott culture.

This case is hardly surprising and may well have been foreseen. It serves as an illuminating example of how a change in management behaviour can itself become a difficult-to-quantify CSF.

Critical success factors are statements of what must be achieved to support each statement of strategic intent. They describe successful and necessary outcomes for the organization. They are not operating plans but, rather, objectives which in turn generate the compilation of operating plans.

Core competencies

This is the last of the characteristics of our successful modern strategy, though in building the strategy it may well not be the last consideration but among the first. It has to do with the organization's properties, strengths and capabilities, and it addresses three questions:

- What are the skills and competencies we have as an organization *now*?

- What are the skills and competencies we will need for the *future*?
- How do we *obtain or develop* that which we do not have?

We need to take a look at what we mean by competencies for they may range in importance from the no longer relevant, at one end of the spectrum, to the source of our competitive advantage, at the other end of the spectrum. There will also be a heavy cluster around the centre which has to do with the good governance of the organization, and there will be some uniquely necessary for the organization to play in a given industry.

Most managers have some familiarity with the core competencies philosophy through SWOT (Strengths, Weaknesses, Opportunities and Threats) analyses which organizations quite commonly conduct upon themselves.

I find it quite useful to think about core competencies in three categories: generic, industry specific and components of competitive advantage.

1 *Generic competencies* – those competencies without which no serious organization can imagine continuing. This would embrace things like:
   (a) Continuous quality improvement.
   (b) Continuous process improvement.
   (c) Continuous customer satisfaction improvement.
   (d) The ability to change fast.
   (e) The ability to learn fast.

In other words competencies which an organization has to have institutionalized or systematized so that they continue to happen.

2 *Industry specific* – competencies which are necessary for the organization to participate in the industry:
   (a) Airlines must have (among other things) aeroplane flying competencies and aircraft maintenance competencies.
   (b) Car dealerships must be able to repair cars.
   (c) Supermarkets must have logistical competencies to keep their shelves filled.

(d) Financial services organizations must be able to assess and manage risk, they must have investment management competencies.

. . . and so on.

Again it must be a systemic part of the organization's day-to-day operation that these competencies are developed, nurtured, improved, expanded, updated or whatever is required for them to operate at or above the industry benchmarks.

3 *Components of competitive advantage* – these are competencies which consistently enable the organization to outperform its competitors:
  (a) Honda's competence to make excellent small engines is believed to set it apart from other manufacturers. It has enabled the company to enter surprising fields for a car manufacturer, e.g. lawn mowers, generators. This competence apparently derives from its days as a motor cycle manufacturer.
  (b) Sony's ability to miniaturize electronic systems and to make them proof against being moved about is a competence which, for example, allowed them to conceive and make the Walkman. The company's competence here dates from its early successes with transistor radios.
  (c) Marks & Spencer's ability to control its production processes to provide consistent quality at acceptable cost. This means that the company rarely leads on price but appears to be able to retain above industry margins.

A core competency is a collection of skills, knowledge, systems and abilities which enable the organization consistently to achieve certain outcomes which are important for its competitive position.

If we bring together the two axes on which we have discussed the subject so far we get a competence matrix as shown below.

Core com- petence	which we have now . . .	and which we will need for the future . . .	which we do not have and will need . . .
Generic			
Industry specific			
A potential source of competitive advantage			

Trying to complete this matrix is a way to focus the organization's attention on the need to build and adapt the shape of the organization, how it is set up to do what it has to, what it needs to add to its portfolio of competencies and, possibly, what it needs to jettison as well. This exercise will prove surprisingly difficult to do.

Taking the first step of determining the existing core competencies will, when you trawl through the organization, lead everybody to adduce their specific area of expertise as a core competency. Resolving an organization-wide set of definitions of core competencies is a contentious activity; filling the boxes in the competence matrix takes time to mull over and agree.

Among those things which often emerge is the realization that the organization may wish or need to deploy access to core competencies differently. In other words this leads to two sets of considerations:

● Potential for outsourcing certain areas of the organiza- tion either to reduce costs or, and there is good precedent for this belief, to improve the quality of the competence by making it free standing and self- sufficient.

- Realizing that it may not be feasible to develop the competence within the existing organizational structure for reasons of time, expense or simply lack of focus, it may make sense to start looking for partners, acquisitions, or access to networks.

It is often, almost usually, the case that the acquisition of or updating of core competencies become a series of critical success factors in an organization's strategy.

Help

↳

Four components of modern strategy

Strategic purpose – what the organization is here to do:
– to provide an outcome for customers
– danger of being fixed on current products/services
– clarity of purpose = good long-term prognosis

Strategic intent – where we will concentrate our energies so that we can deliver purpose long term.

A series of statements collectively outlining strategic intent; describes the positioning of the organization in relation to markets:
– focuses on the future
– which industry; industries merging and emerging
– what is the future of the industry; how will it be affected by customers, globalization, competitors and technology
– where can we add value; future profit at different points in the value chain
– what financial aspirations we seek

Strategic intent, vision and organizational values – when jointly determined provide an overall frame of reference for employees

Critical success factors – those things which have to go right to achieve our strategic intent:
– what has to be achieved not how it is to be done
– can be start of the planning exercise
– must command organization effort hence must be critical
– sometimes they are fuzzy

Core competencies – what strengths will we have to develop:
– competency is a collection of skills, knowledge, systems and abilities enabling certain outcomes
– generic; needed by all organizations
– industry specific; needed to operate in the industry
– source of competitive advantage
– need to assess *now*, *maintain* and *need for future*

6 Developing your strategy

The story so far

If you are working sequentially through this book, by now you will have:

- an understanding of what organizational strategy is (Help Screens at the end of Chapters 1 and 2)
- an overview of those things which are driving the operating environment of the modern organization (Help Screen at the end of Chapter 3)
- an understanding of how these 'environmental drivers' affect traditional organizational strategies and some advice on what a viable contemporary strategy might concern itself with (Help Screen at the end of Chapter 5).

What we now need to turn to is a series of practical steps which will enable you, as a line manager, to start the process of building a strategy.

Who should be developing the strategy

The central thesis of this book is that:

- strategy should be developed at all levels within the organization from top team down
- the line manager, the supervisor or head of a department, the leader of a team, the manager of the function (whatever the unit of construction of the organization)

must become a strategist if he or she and the unit are to provide the organization with value

● the development of strategy should involve the input and shaping of all members of the organization so that it can access the unique benefit of contribution from the line, from the in-depth knowledge all employees can bring to the strategy-building process based on their detailed understanding how the organization actually works, – the 'employee or line manager reality test' as we have called it elsewhere.

Incidentally to save the need for constant definition we will use the word 'unit' to mean department, team, functional division or whatever. The defining characteristic is that a person, the line manager, has responsibility for the output of the unit and for the members who operate within it.

How we will build the strategy

The organizing principle behind building the strategy will be the four-part process (purpose, strategic intent, critical success factors and core competencies) we have been using so far. We will spend more time on strategic intent than any other part of the strategy, and in doing so we will successively refine the first pass we make at defining it so that we can test and test again the implications of our thinking.

Critical success factors and core competencies will lead us into the area of implementation and action planning.

Components of the strategy development process

Figure 6.1 is a diagrammatic map of the development process. We will use this map to orientate us through the whole process.

Strategic intent is the largest area of strategy development, and so Chapters 8, 9, 10 and 11 state it, test it and, finally, agree it ready for critical success factors.

Figure 6.1

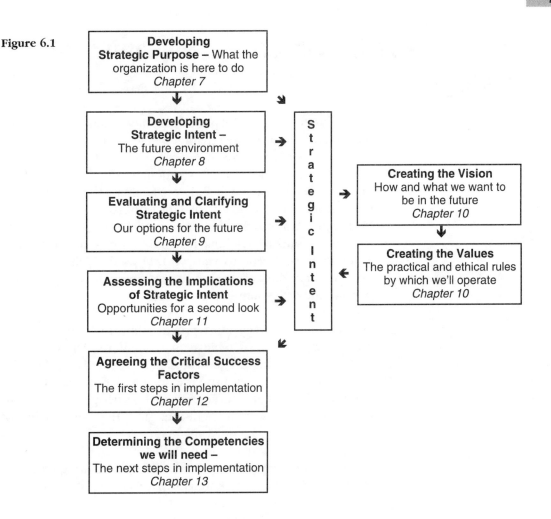

You may find the placing of the vision and values components slightly unexpected. Many people consider that vision and values are the absolute starting point of developing a strategy. I hold the view that building vision and values is more securely anchored in reality if we have first thought about the future and our potential role in it. There is no reason why you should not start with the Vision and Values Activities if you feel that they will serve you better.

Throughout we are taking a future perspective. We are not trying to be fortune-tellers or soothsayers; we are trying to make logical deductions about the future and we are doing so based on what we know of the major drivers of change we have dealt with in Chapter 3.

The process by which we will build the strategy

In each of the component parts of the development process we will be advising a set of Activities, some of which are designed to take place in a workshop environment. In developing these Activities I have taken care to set them within the scope of the line manager to enable him or her to facilitate the workshop. In other words you should not miss the opportunities provided to lead your team through the development process. You should not have to seek professional facilitation nor be reliant on your Training Department to run workshops for you. If you do choose that route, however, make sure you are an active participant with your people.

Developing a strategy must provide time for participants to mull over what they achieve in workshops. There is huge merit in providing a good balance between pacing the development fairly swiftly on the one hand, but separating the component parts of it sufficiently so that people have time to reflect on their own conclusions and the conclusions of others.

To help orientate you and provide examples as we go through the process, we are tracking two parallel case studies:

- The Acme IT team – a relatively new department in a smallish, medium- to low-technology engineering company. The IT team provides us with an example of an internal company department or functional division – a unit – getting to grips with building a strategy.
- Magnum Motors – a car dealership for an up-market make of car which is much coveted as a success symbol. Magnum is plotting a strategy for the whole company and the work you see in the case studies is the work of the top team.

The approach, and indeed the culture, of the two case study entities is very different. The material is provided so that you can see the range of acceptable responses to the Activities and to surmise the degree to which a 'unit strategy' differs in nature from a 'whole organization' strategy. Outcomes are different; the process for generating it is not.

Involvement

Again a plea . . .

Nothing will contribute more to the unit or to the organization operating more strategically, and hence more effectively, than involving its members in developing the strategy. The information and opinions you will access will be better; the creativity and originality you will tap will be better; and, finally, involvement will start the process change for which you will be looking.

Good luck!

7 Developing strategic purpose

Figure 7.1

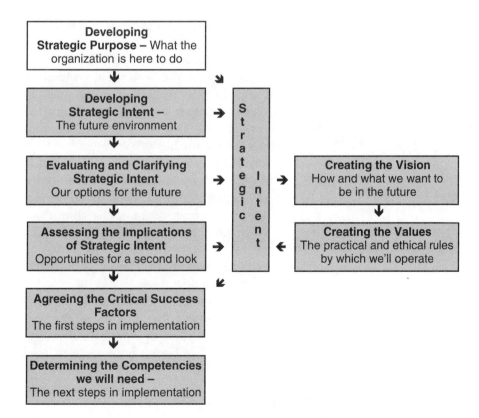

What this chapter should achieve

- It will enable a thoughtful exploration of the long-term contribution of your unit and/or your organization.
- If you involve others, colleagues, staff, bosses or customers, you will achieve a level of consensus and agreement about the purpose of the unit and/or your organization.
- Since this is the start of the strategy development exercise, you will get a taste of the style and type of thinking you will be involved in as the process proceeds.
- The output will be a statement, or perhaps more than one, which describes the unit's and the organization's purpose or purposes.

The process

- We will use a questionnaire-prompting technique designed to explore different facets of the unit's activities.
- The process will start from simple headline type approaches. It will then diverge to explore more detail and, finally, converge again into a purpose statement, or series of statements.
- You could design a workshop around this format, or you could have a number of informed stakeholders doing it independently and then get together for debriefing and discussion. However you do it, remember that involving the stakeholders will improve the quality of your results by having drawn on more brains and canvassed more points of view. You will also have whetted stakeholders' appetites for further involvement.
- Your results may not be phrased in mellifluous prose at the end of the exercise and this is not important. The really important thing to achieve from the group is a shared and common understanding of what you have collectively said. Delay the wordsmithing until what you have developed undergoes the reality test of people having thought about it more and tested it more as the process goes on.
- Your may not reach agreement or consensus as a group. This complicates the process in that you will have to carry the 'outrider' opinions further down the process until (as is most likely) they resolve themselves.

Here is the first set of Activities you should undertake to establish purpose.

7.1 Determining strategic purpose

1 Describe the products and services your unit currently provides.

2 Define the customers or classes of customers to whom you provide the products or services.

3 Describe the benefits which the customer(s) gain from the products or services.

4 Describe the expectations of quality each category of customer expects from each product or service.

> Here is what the preliminary pass at Activity 5.1 produced for the IT team at Acme. The example, of course, covers a unit application.

Acme IT team

Question 1 Products and services supplied

- Communication systems: e-mail, word processing.
- Work improvement systems: spreadsheeting, d-base, diaries, company product specifications.
- Specialized functional systems: accounting, inventory control, job costing.

Question 2 Customers or classes of customers

- Employees of Acme Corp.
- External 'stakeholders'; clients, suppliers, auditors.

Question 3 Benefits gained by customers

- Productivity improvement.
- Improved accuracy/quality of information.
- Improved appearance of documents.

Question 4 Expectations of quality

- User-friendly system interface/ease of operation.
- High reliability – no lost data.
- Speed of system response.
- No downtime.

Here is the response produced by the top team at Magnum Motors who were developing a strategy for their organization:

Magnum Motors top team

Question 2 Customers or classes of customer

Magnum handled this question first which enabled them to produce the following matrix relating all questions to each class of customer.

The public in our geographical area Social class B and C1 People wanting a visible statement of wealth/success Corporate buyers	The owners of Magnum and major shareholders	The Manufacturer (i.e. the makers of the cars for which Magnum was the franchisee/dealership)	The staff of Magnum

Question 1 Products/services provided

Public	Owners	Manufacturer	Staff
Cars, light vans Finance facilities Service and repair of vehicles	Capital growth Dividend Opportunity of investment	Local marketing and selling	Employment Training

Question 3 Benefits gained by customers

Public	Owners	Manufacturer	Staff
Comfortable, high-performance motoring Prestige/status FRFT,* high-quality service	Higher rates of capital growth than you'd find elsewhere Reasonable security	Cash flow High unit sales Maintain the brand image High customer satisfaction	Fair pay Good perks Some career development Reasonable security

Question 4 Expectations of quality

Public	Owners	Manufacturer	Staff
Trouble-free motoring Ethical selling Immaculate vehicle condition Considerate consultative servicing	Higher (than now) increase in shareholder value Greater potential for Magnum to make them rich	Continued top ranking Customer Satisfaction Index Readiness to take new (smaller car) line	Good physical surroundings Mentor/coach type approach to management More/better career development and training

Note: *FRFT means fix right first time.

Let us stop for a moment and reflect on what has surfaced in this exercise.

Acme IT team

Even at this early stage the IT team was surprised because their thinking had shifted from a purpose which, though unarticulated, was thought to be 'provision and maintenance of IT-related systems'. Their new reality arose as a result of moving from the *product* (IT services) fixation to *the benefits of the product*. This revised the way they saw their purpose to: 'productivity improvement, accuracy and quality of appearance'.

Magnum Motors

Magnum was not surprised by this first-part purpose exercise. Because they were a top team, they had come to grips some time ago with the idea of having a number of different 'customers' – the organizational accountability model we saw in Chapter 3.

Magnum's primary concern was financial. The top team, between them, owned more than half of the dealership; their interest was to expand the shareholder value so that they could all become rich. The expansion capacity of the business was, as we shall see, limited.

Gleaning the information from the first pass is important. Not surprisingly this information is often greeted with: 'Well we all knew that, of course.' This may or may not be true, but it has been my experience that whether known or not, day-to-day decisions the departments or organizations have taken can usually be shown to reflect priorities quite other than purpose. It is also usually possible to demonstrate that recent or forthcoming decisions may not necessarily be the same if considered in the light of the primacy of purpose.

Now let us diverge slightly to examine the information in more depth. Here we are looking at actual and potential competitors, different ways of delivering the benefits, ways in which the customers might change.

We are also trying to define the territory in which you might build a competitive advantage. In doing this we are anticipating some of the questions we are going to have to handle on the strategic intent section. We are doing this now because it just might affect the way in which we are thinking about purpose.

7.2 Relating strategic purpose to a future environment

1 *Consider who else provides the benefits which the unit has identified as being at the heart of its purpose?*
Comparatively how do you stack up against each other? What are their greatest strengths, things they do better than you? What are the things you do better than them?

2 *Stretching your imagination, who else might provide these benefits?*
Why are they not providing them now?
What might cause them to provide these benefits in the future?

3 *Again stretching your imagination, how might these benefits be provided by a means other than the way in which you are providing them? (Think technology, for example.)*

4 *Will your customers be requiring the benefits you provide in the longer term? Will your customers still be there in the long term or might they vanish? Why?*

5 *What do you perceive as your greatest intrinsic strengths in providing these benefits?*
What are your greatest vulnerabilities?

Here are the responses of our chosen cases.

Acme IT team

Question 1 Who else provides the service? How you better? How they better?

External bureaus could provide services:

- they might be slower than we are
- understand less about our business.

On the other hand they:

- would have more available expertise to adapt, programme
- they might also be cheaper than the all-up cost of our department
- through dial-up diagnostics they might be faster than we are.

Question 2 Who else might provide benefits – why?

If Acme were sold, a new corporate headquarters might provide the service.

Question 3 Might the benefits be provided in the future by another means?

Generic software *could* become so friendly and easy to use, we might not be needed – employees could figure it out for themselves.

Question 4 Will your customers be requiring the benefits you provide long term?

Again, if Acme were sold this whole site could vanish.

Question 5 Your strengths? Your vulnerabilities?

Our strengths are:

- our knowledge of the business
- our relationships with the customers
- our good track record.

Our vulnerabilities are:

- that we are or may be more expensive than external suppliers
- we do not have enough unique expertise for an acquiring company to preserve us in the case of a company sale.

What has now emerged?

The Acme IT department

At Acme two categories of new and important consideration have emerged:

1 Purpose has not changed a great deal as a result of Activity 7.2, relating purpose to the future – it still remains *improvement in productivity, accuracy, quality of appearance*. What has been added are:

   (a) the need to achieve this improvement at prices lower than the service could be bought outside

   (b) the need to build the expertise of the department so that it can compete at a competence level with both the external bureau and the centralized corporate division should Acme be sold.

2 The IT department needs to do a lot more information-gathering; is the cost of the department more expensive than an external bureau would be? Could the bureau respond as fast as the department does?

In principle then the unwordsmithed purpose statement would subsume all of the following:

- improvement in productivity, accuracy and quality of appearance
- at a cost to the organization comparable to, or better than can be bought externally
- providing fast access to a high degree of IT or related expertise.

In reality when the strategy-building exercise was completed by the IT department on which this case is based, the purpose statement had moved some distance beyond the concept of productivity improvement. The team finally saw its purpose as providing some of the means of competitive advantage to Acme; we will see this emerge in subsequent Activities.

In turn, as one might imagine, this radically changed the range of products and services the team had originally identified. Further, because it had also accepted as part of its purpose that it would operate at or below the cost of external bureaus, this changed its view of the core competencies it needed to develop.

Magnum Motors

The team chose to handle the Activity as an extended discussion which they minuted as follows:

1 Our current business is in good nic (*sic*), our CSI* is the best in the business. The manufacturer will not appoint another distributor in our territory, and if XXX (another named competitor manufacturer) did, it would not damage us severely because customers are already mobile anyway.
2 A time will come when the internal combustion engine will be unacceptable but that's for the manufacturer to worry about.
3 There will always be a need for no hassle, prestige luxury motoring.
4 Our core problem is that we cannot grow the business fast enough to satisfy our shareholders and our strategy has to be about:

  • maintaining our present business in the excellent shape it is in
  • finding a means of growing it, or growing a new business.

Note: *CSI = Customer Satisfaction Index, an index specified by the manufacturer, fed by data collected by the manufacturer and applied across all dealerships. Magnum's CSI is best in class for the manufacturer.

Magnum Motors

Magnum's first-pass purpose statement was:

  • To provide the highest quality service for the prestige motorist.
  • To perform consistently at the top end of all manufacturer's CSI.
  • To grow the business so that shareholder value is increased rapidly.

Developing a *strategic purpose statement* means:

- moving your thinking from products and services to customer benefits
- re-examining the context of customer benefits by looking at:
  - who else, long term, might provide the benefit and why
  - whether the benefit, long term, will still be needed
  - whether the benefit will be provided, long term, in the same way as it is now
- writing up your purpose statement as simply as possible; lots of verbs and hard-edged definers added as bullet points.

8 Developing strategic intent: the future environment

Figure 8.1

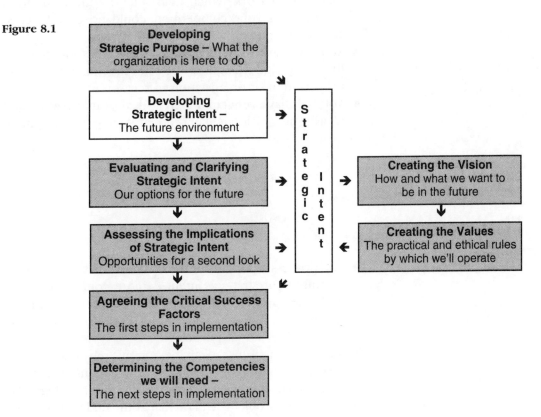

As you can see from Figure 8.1, we now move into the first phase of developing strategic intent specifically looking at the future environment in which we will be operating.

This is one of the longer exercises in developing strategic intent and covers no less than six Activities, all of which are important.

At the end of the chapter you will have a lot of loose ends and Chapter 9 will help you knit them all together again.

What this chapter should achieve

- At the end of this section you will have created a picture of the general environment in which you believe you will be operating in the future.
- You will have mastered a model called the *competitive forces framework* which helps identify the main areas from which your competition could arise and hence around which you will build your strategy.
- You will have examined each of the areas identified in the model and thought of the relevance to, and position of, your unit or organization in relation to it.
- You will have generated a great deal of information and ideas which will feed subsequent strategy development processes.

The process

- The process of looking at the future so that you can start to build your strategic intent is more complicated than was the process of establishing strategic purpose. Importantly, though, you cannot establish intent until you are clear about purpose.
- Again we will use Activities with questionnaires to prompt our thinking. It is possible to accomplish the six Activities in this section with your group in a single day. One of the problems will be that at the end of it we seem

to have a number of loose ends so if it is possible you should set up the session so that you can cover the content of Chapter 9 as well. A day and a half would be good, but you could do it faster.

- For the first Activity in this section we provide an example from Magnum Motors. It is in Chapter 9, however, that you get a fuller picture of how our two cases responded to the 'Determining the future environment' Activities. It is in Chapter 9 that the output of these exercises comes together so that is the more appropriate place to show the case results, but look ahead to them if you like.

- Do not be dismayed if you feel you do not have all the information necessary to do justice to the Activities – at least it will provide you with a list of things you have to gather information about or think about more.

- Finally, let me make the now predictable remark about involvement. The more you involve your people, the better the information you will get and the better you will have teed up the change processes which will follow.

Determining the future

Impudent as such a concept is, you have to take a view, so here goes.

8.1 Describing the future environment

It is assumed that this will take place in a workshop environment facilitated by the line manager or team leader in charge.

Step 1 *Get your group together and explain the Activity.*

Step 2 *Have people work individually on the prompts to get an overall idea of the Activity.*

Step 3 *Then put them into syndicate groups and assign each of the key headings to a group (a group can handle more than one if there are* not many people). Allow a fair amount of time – more than half an hour per key heading – in the syndicates so that you cause an informed conversation to take place.

Step 4   Take feedback from each group, generate discussion around each area and capture the results for later circulation.

Steps 5 to 10   Each of the successive Activities in this chapter provide a page of trigger questions for your group. Use each set of trigger questions to set up either a plenary or syndicate exercise as above.

You can have syndicates working in parallel on Activities 8.2–8.6 if you wish but it is always good sense to vary the members of syndicates and to change the subject emphasis around.

Once you are familiar with all six Activities in this chapter, you will certainly find the best way to use them.

Above all remember to capture all the information your groups generate – all of it is employed as we synthesize and evaluate in Chapter 9.

Use the following to trigger Activity 8.1.

Place yourself five years in the future and make notes under each of the following topic areas.

1 Law and regulation
How will changes in the law, national, EU or other, have affected the industry, the organization and the unit in which you operate?
How will changes in government policy have affected the industry, the organization and the unit in which you operate?
If your industry is subject to a regulator, what effect will that have had?
How will industry standards have changed things?

2 Economy

What will the economy which underlies your industry's health or your unit's funding be like in five years' time? Think about domestic and world economy.

Will customers have more or less money to spend on the products and services you offer?

3 Technology

What effect will technology have had on your industry in five years?

Think about how products and services will have been changed by technology.

Think about how the products and services are supplied might have changed.

Think about how technology might have changed the marketing, promotion and selling which support the sales of your product or service.

Consider the impact of the Internet.

4 Social and cultural factors

How will changing fashion have affected the products and services you supply?

How will the view of the media have affected your products and services?

How will pressure groups, e.g. environmental groups, have affected your industry?

5 Staff and skills

Will your industry be attracting people who want to work in it?

Will they have the requisite skills, will you have to train?

Will people be relatively more or less expensive than they are now?

How will their views be affecting the way your organization operates?

The results of a first pass at this exercise will usually generate a bulleted picture of the future which, if it has been a collective exercise, is supported by a high degree of agreement and concurrence.

Here is an edited example of a first pass at this exercise developed by the senior management team at Magnum Motors.

Legislation
Company car driver liable to heavier taxation – engine size.
Road charges and road usage restrictions – tolls.
Questions on sustainability of licensed dealerships in guaranteed territories.
New rules on scrappage which will up list price and disposal cost.

Economy
Interest charges likely to remain high foreseeably.
Economic downturn foreseen post-2000, with recovery not until 2003, will disproportionately impact the luxury car – both corporate and private sale.
Poor industry reputation in the City means investment cash is hard to find.

Technology
The car increasingly high-tech:

– lengthening service intervals (i.e. lower lifetime revenue)
– requiring greater service skills (higher training cost, constant retraining).

New marketing techniques emerging – highly targeted.
Database availability of used cars is reducing the competitive advantage of the well-stocked second-hand car lot.

Social and cultural factors
Probable increasing criticism levelled at the big car.
The industry (especially second-hand part of it) has a poor public image.
Environmental lobbies and the car – emissions, recycling, fossil fuels etc.

Staff and skills
Again, poor industry reputation, harder to attract good people.
Consistent need for expensive service training.

This case is the almost complete transcription of a forty-minute exercise conducted with two syndicates; it does not pretend to completeness but serves as an example of an acceptable starting point.

The exercise fails if what emerges is simply an extrapolation of the present. Few, indeed probably no, industries or businesses are static or even changing slowly. If people believe things are relatively static they are usually ignoring the lessons of the immediate past and determinedly myopic about the future.

One of the greatest problems that all organizations face is that managers, at all levels, are taking insufficient time to research and imagine the future. Concerned as line managers all are with 'keeping the show on the road', the opportunities for long-think do not naturally exist.

Organizations which do not make space for such considerations are doomed to a reactive role rather than taking charge of the future.

Nor is it necessarily sufficient for the management of the organization to construct the future scenario; many organizations find it valuable, and sometimes vital, to look outside for information and help.

Demographers, think tanks, academics, futurologists, all have their role to play even if only to provoke management into serious thinking about the future.

Activity 8.1 and the evolving picture of the future it paints provides a background to the really core issues we have to address as strategists. The fact that it is background does not render it unimportant, rather it provides context against which the core issues of customers and competitors take greater relevance.

Determining the competitive environment of the future

We switch to looking more closely at competition, what governs it and hence where we might mark out our own particular territory; our choice of battlefield, if you like. Remember not to lose sight of the future, five-years-on perspective while you grapple with competitive forces.

To help understand this let us take a look at an important graphic, the competitive forces framework (Figure 8.2), which describes the framework in which competition arises. The source is our friend Michael Porter whom we encountered in Chapter 2.

Figure 8.2
Competitive forces framework

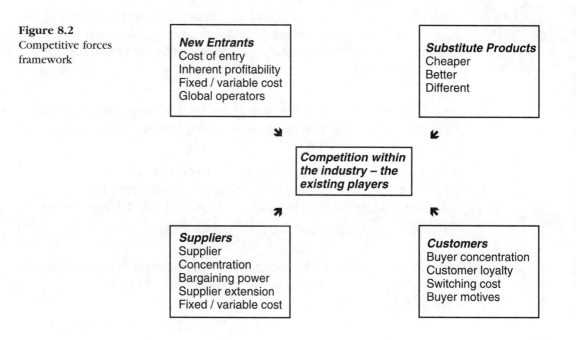

Porter's competitive forces matrix leads us into a five-part Activity in which we examine each of the boxes in detail and relate their significance to our unit.

Competition within the industry: the existing players (the middle box)

We have already seen the scenario of an existing group of competitors, competing for similar markets passing a share of the market from one to another as each develops a marginal competitive edge. We have also seen that ultimately this makes nobody especially profitable and hence does not persist for too long. What causes it to change is the redefinition of the market, i.e. when one competitor changes the basis of the primary buying motive in a way which others cannot easily replicate.

In predicting how the existing competitors will perform in the future a useful concept is the *intensity of investment* in the industry. To make a metre of a synthetic fibre, you need a substantial investment in chemical and spinning plant. A metre of silk fibre on the other hand just needs a silk worm and some mulberry leaves. Synthetic fibre manufacturers must then compete aggressively for markets because of their investment. Silk spinners have not nearly so much at stake.

Hard-edged considerations like investment are of course important, but remember emotional issues like loyalty to staff, tradition, importance to local communities etc. All have an effect on whether competitors will continue the competitive slugging match. Sometimes competition persists well beyond the reasonable. The British car industry, for example, took an unconscionable time to die and even if it did fight its competitive corner increasingly unconvincingly, it was none the less a competitor.

Thinking about your competition five years on also means that you must make some judgements on the intrinsic excellence or quality of competitors' organizations. Companies which have a successful track record at changing fast, moving into and out of markets rapidly, have obviously to be taken as more serious or, at least, less predictable competition.

Two final remarks at opposite ends of the spectrum of potential relationships need to be made and need to be seriously considered by the strategist:

- Today's competitors are tomorrow's potential partners.
- Remember strategy is about winning wars – no strategic plan should lose sight of the need to beat the competition, victory could be by successful engagement, but remember the judgement of Sun Tzu, the great Chinese strategist we quoted in Chapter 1: '100 victories in 100

battles is not the pinnacle of excellence. Subjugating the enemy's army without fighting is the true pinnacle of excellence.'

We call this trick *market redefinition* or *corporate reinvention*.

Assessing competition within the industry: the existing players (middle box)

8.2 Assessing existing competition

Think about your main competitors now, those we have described as 'existing players'. We want to try to assess the importance of each five years on from now.

You might try to compile a matrix to enable comparisons; however you do it you need to give serious consideration to the following for **each named competitor***:*

- *What is their current market share or importance in the market?*
- *Will they be there in five years' time? In thinking about this consider:*

  - *How profitable are they or how important is the profitability of this area of competition in relation to their total profitability?*
  - *Assess the intensity of their investment.*
  - *Is there an emotional attachment to the market?*
  - *Do they play in this market as an extension of their core activities, or is it their core activity?*
  - *What advantages would there be in their continuing in the market or in withdrawing from it?*

- *What are their competitive advantages in relation to yours? E.g. They're better at . . .; We're better at . . . Think from the customer's perspective.*

- *In thinking about their competitive advantages consider whether there is merit in partnering with them? Merit for you, merit for them.*
- *In thinking about their competitive advantage, how best could you nullify the advantage? Again think client perspective, but also think **changing** the game not only **getting better** at it.*
- *Assess how likely this competitor is to affect, influence or redefine the market. Place them, for example, on a scale of 1 to 5, a **reactor (1)** or a **reinventor (5)**? That will provide a danger index. Then think why or how they would do it.*
- *Be frank with yourself and ask yourself if you really know enough about each competitor. Where would you go for more information? How would you get to learn about their strategy?*
- *Finally, consider whether you really have **all the current competitors** on the list and whether you know enough about each of them. If your organization is typical, you will know much less than you need to.*

Determining the competitive environment of the future: new entrants (the top-left box)

One of the things which attracts a new entrant to a market will be the perception of the amount of money it believes it can make. But such a decision is also tempered by the other important consideration of what it will cost to enter the market. Here, to further refine the rules, we have also to consider whether entering that market is an extension of the potential competitor's business or a new departure. Extensions are generally cheaper than new departures. So, for example, while it was presumably expensive for Marks & Spencer to enter the food market, it was a great deal cheaper for them to do so than it would have been for an organization without an existing presence in the high streets of Britain.

Another example is that of new magazines which are constantly appearing because it is relatively inexpensive for a magazine publisher to extend into a different market once it has editorial expertise, printing and distribution in position. In other words, entry into a new market segment is at variable cost; it is not necessary to make the huge initial investment, merely the investment associated with the specific task involved.

One of the characteristics of the Internet is that it enables anybody to reach, at extremely low cost, one of the world's largest markets. Further, that market is self-selecting in that it searches for information which it specifies. Coupled to this is the international transactional infrastructure provided by credit cards enabling people to buy where they please. These factors combine to lower the cost of whole areas of market entry to a virtual nil.

Among the most difficult things for the strategist to guess at is who, in a predatory global economy, new competitors might be. Frequently the new entrant will be a global player one may never even have heard of let alone seriously considered as a competitor. National governments in their search for inward investment and job creation are frequently building bridge-heads into markets which change the competitive environment significantly.

Global competitive invasion is often far less observed in that substitute products are marketed by national suppliers frequently under their own brand. My last pair of Marks & Spencer shoes were made in Thailand, a fact which might or might not have been anticipated in Leicester, the shoe-making capital of the UK.

New entrants (top-left box)

8.3 New competitors: new entrants to the markets

We want, in this Activity, to look beyond the existing competitors at the potential competitive environment.

While this Activity is part of the extended awayday advised in Activity 8.1, another way of handling this is to do a brainstorm with an informed group of colleagues, employees and, even, customers.

While the trigger questions here are phrased in terms more appropriate to a total organization strategy – think, too, about new entrants outside the company who might provide an interesting alternative to an in-house operation.

First clues – likelihood of new entrants

- *How profitable is this industry/market anyway? . . . and how fast is it growing?*
- *Is it expensive to enter the industry/market? Capital investment to develop products/services, cost of distribution etc.?*
- *Have new players entered the industry or the market recently? Where did they come from? Related industries, offshore entrants?*
- *Return to Activity 8.1 and consider how some of the broader future developments of legislation, technology, social and cultural patterns, and the economy might impact the likelihood of new entrants.*

Second clues – source of new entrants

- *What is the industry wisdom about where new players come from? Which external industries or organizations is your industry most concerned about usually?*
- *List the specific skills/competencies/capabilities a player must have to service these markets. Which industries/market players/organizations have competencies most closely related?*
- *Where (in the world) are these skills and competencies at their best or at least ubiquitous? Who are the international players?*
- *Are there industries or suppliers of goods and services different from those which you supply but who regularly talk to your marketplace?*
- *Are there suppliers of goods and services similar to your own who do not presently talk to your marketplace?*

Third clues – the Internet and its consequences

Having considered seriously the implications of capital investment and entry cost into your markets, how does the Internet change the equation? How will you monitor your vulnerabilities?

Determining the competitive environment of the future: substitute products (the top-right box)

It is Ralph Waldo Emerson who is reputed to have said: 'If a man . . . make a better mousetrap than his neighbour, tho' he build his house in the woods, the world will make a beaten path to his door.'

The serious strategist would be ill advised to accept this assertion as reliable. Porter certainly admits the competitive advantage of the better mousetrap, but he also adds 'cheaper' to the equation. Also, the word 'different' implies solving the mouse problem without recourse to a mousetrap at all.

These product changes can emerge from either the existing industry players, or from new entrants to the market. The strategic planner has got to consider both potential sources and, so, needs to assess competitor or potential competitor capability carefully.

Providing *cheaper products* depends on process improvement, sometimes on capital investment, often on new (potentially global) sourcing either of manufacture or of materials.

Providing *better products* depends on continuous quality improvement, on excellence in design, and often on different use of materials.

Providing *different products* depends on creativity and imagination. It is the stuff of which market redefinition is made. It is often, though not always, the province of a new entrant.

In completing the next Activity, again return to Activity 8.1 and consider especially the potential impact of technology, not only the product or service, but the broader context of the provision of the service. Compact discs (CDs) have replaced tapes which replaced vinyl records; word processors replaced typewriters, PCs replaced accounting machines and so on. The relentless march of technology in the twentieth century makes examples easy to find.

But what the strategist cannot afford to ignore is the potential for a complete conceptual shift. Electronic mail is conceptually remote from the postal services. The contraceptive pill is conceptually remote from the condom. In each of these two examples the benefit is provided by a means different from that which could be achieved by progressive refinement and improvement of the original product. Further, the buying decision, the processes of purchase and the providers of the products are different from those who supplied the original product.

Substitute products (top-right box)

8.4 Thinking about changes in the product/service

This Activity tries to bring some radical thinking to the product/service area of competition.

Potential for 'cheaper'

Most products or services have three or four major cost components which go to make up their retail price. (A book for example is about 20 per cent author and manufacturing, 40 per cent publisher's overhead, 40 per cent booksellers' discount.)

- *Identify the major cost categories of your products or services.*
- *Conduct an exercise to see how you could cut each cost component in half.*
- *What would you have to do to sell the idea of a major list price reduction within the organization?*

Potential for 'better'

- *How good are you as an organization at continuous improvement and continuous innovation? Are you pacing the competitive environment or are you usually in catch-up mode? What would it take to install or develop an effective organizational culture of continuous improvement/innovation?*

- *Conduct a customer survey to discover what 'better' really means in the context of your product or service – look for additional and new ways to add value.*

Potential for 'different'

- *Assess how well informed you think the organization is. Is it up to date with what is happening in the broader world outside of your industry?*
- *Assess your organization's creativity. Is it possible or likely that a radical new product or service approach might surface somewhere in the organization, if so where?*
- *If something innovative did surface, how good would the organization be at seizing the chance it offered?*
- *What might you do to improve the creativity of the organization and to improve the quality or breadth of information with which it is dealing?*

In an in-organization department context, process re-engineering, usually implemented to cut internal costs, can be looked upon in the same light as a different product from the organization's viewpoint.

Determining the competitive environment of the future: customers or buyers (the bottom-right box)

Porter chose to use 'buyer' when he developed the competitive framework, so that the customer's position in the supply chain was evident. We will use the words 'customer' and 'buyer' interchangeably, thus reminding ourselves of the activity of buying, while not losing sight of the overtones of satisfaction inherent in the organization or unit's relationship with its customer.

Among the most important things for the strategist to consider is how your customer, your buyer will be behaving in the future. When we looked at purpose we established that it is not products or services you are supplying to the customer but benefits. Focusing on this benefits approach inevitably opens your mind to all the potential developments in this competitive framework scenario. It is, however, most important when you train your sights on the customer of the future.

First let us dispense with the chimera of customer loyalty; while it is a factor, it is a more reliably predicted phenomenon when it is considered in terms of *switching costs*. The customer's continued disposition to buy from you will depend more on the cost or difficulty of using an alternative supplier than it will on any natural predisposition to you. The closer the product or service is to a commodity, the lower the switching cost, buying decisions in the commodity area are usually dominated by considerations of price. When we buy fuel for the car, supplier A's petrol is likely to be identical to supplier B's; we will thus shop for price, convenience or both. Converting the car to petroleum gas, however, though it will provide great long-term economy, means that we have a high switching cost and are thus unlikely to do so unless for a very compelling reason.

How, then, can you raise the switching cost to the customer? Go back to Chapter 2, where we discussed Theodore Levitt's total product concept, to refresh your ideas. The more the product is specifically versioned for the customer, the more it exceeds the expected and enters the realm of the potential, the higher the switching cost and the higher the demonstration of customer 'loyalty'.

The kind of thinking outlined above is fairly well focused on the present scheme of things and on the expectation that:

- the customer will continue to require the same benefit longer term
- the benefit will be delivered in substantially the same way as it is now.

Neither of these expectations is necessary reliable, and may be a distraction from the reality of the situation. You can improve carbon ribbon efficiency, price and availability to the perfect but nobody will buy carbon ribbons for printers which now operate on laser or ink jet technology.

While we looked at 'different' in the substitute product category; we need also to look at 'different' in the context of the customer. Technological change aside, buying decisions will be affected by customers' motives. These are sometimes a great deal harder to project long term for they are also affected by fashion, by current belief systems, by the reputation of the industry and so on.

Manipulating those intangibles can become part of the strategy. Body Shop's eco-friendliness and animal testing aversion could be described as a value (see later) but it could also be seen as a conscious strategy. It must be said that the causes of eco-friendliness and anti-animal testing are much advanced by the publicity and prominence Body Shop accords to its business conduct in both areas. Either way you look at it Body Shop has identified a buyer motive which is standing it in good stead and catching competitors on the back foot with everybody having to demonstrate their compliance with these buyer motives.

Our hard-working strategist will think, too, about customer's possible moves to control the market. Buying collectives can and do occur, forcing prices down and liberalizing supply terms like credit and delivery.

8.5 Customers'/buyers' future behaviour and motivation

Earlier we have done some thinking about the buyer so refresh yourself with a look at the material you have already developed on the customer.

What we should get out of this Activity is a guess at customer behaviour five years on.

Remember, think benefits, not products or services.

Demographics etc.
- *What do we know about the demographics of the market(s)? Will the customers who make up the market be older, younger, fewer, more numerous?*

- *Will they be richer or poorer?*
- *Will you still be talking to them through the same media you are talking to them now?*
- *Will you be supplying them through the same channels?*
- *Where will you go to get reliable answers to the questions above?*

Buying motives and criteria

- *Will the benefit your product/service currently provides still be sought by the customers? How can you be sure?*
- *How will fashion, public opinion, lobbies, pressure groups and legislation have affected buying motives?*
- *Speculate on what the customer will expect as a baseline set of criteria for a buying decision – quality, durability, choice, delivery, after sales etc.*

Loyalty and switching costs

- *Is there potential to increase the switching cost to the customer without alienating him or her? Think versioning, adding perceived value; Levitt's potential product.*
- *How will your competitors be confronting the switching cost issue?*

You may find that some of the material here is difficult to categorize as 'product based' or 'customer based' – do not worry, we will find a way of integrating and evaluating what you have surfaced in a sensible way.

Determining the competitive environment of the future: suppliers (the bottom-left box)

Just as your unit or industry has customers so, too, it has suppliers who are important in the competitive equation in that you are dependent upon them and therefore, in the longer term, you must predict how they will behave.

The general rule is that the more suppliers there are to the industry the less power each wields. Multiple suppliers by competing with each other tend to keep prices down, deliver and supply more flexibly, and often offer longer credit. If there are relatively few suppliers to the industry they are capable of exercising great influence to the point that a monopolist supplier exercises absolute power.

Again the strategist must consider the likely developments in the supplier industry. What happens if suppliers amalgamate and, therefore, are in a more monopolistic position. Should special relationships be set up with selected suppliers, should new suppliers be sourced and so on?

Remember, too, that your suppliers will be conducting on you the Activity you have just conducted upon your customers. In other words they will be speculating on your long-term buying motives, on how to raise switching costs to you, on how to add what you perceive to be value. They will also be concerned that you and your competitors might start to concentrate buying and thus force down their prices or margins.

Increasingly we see alliances between suppliers and customers being created as part of the strategy of both. We also see organizations outsourcing activities, usually for cost purposes, which have previously been conducted internally. If that becomes part of a strategy, assuring continuity of supply probably becomes a critical success factor.

Japanese organizations have been particularly effective in managing their suppliers. Toyota intrudes with great depth into its suppliers' businesses, dictating not only highly detailed product specification, and, indeed, even the processes by which the product will be made, but also controlling supplier margins and selling prices. This level of intrusion is accepted because it can be balanced against not only a higher degree of financial security but also by access to the expertise of Toyota.

Suppliers (bottom-left box)

8.6 Assessing supplier behaviour in the future

This Activity will help you assess whether, long term, you are vulnerable to supplier pressure and thus help you develop a strategy to deal with it.

Identifying critical suppliers

Identify those products or services you buy which are critical to the operation of your organization or unit. (Typically these will be raw materials and component suppliers, particular expertise you buy outside etc. It can also be the landlord if your location is critical, so think widely but deal only with those suppliers which are strategically important.)

Assessing vulnerability

For each strategically important supplier you have identified deal with the following questions:

- *Are there many/few suppliers now?*
- *Five years on will there be more/fewer? Think amalgamations and acquisitions, new entrants.*
- *Is the financial health of the supplier industry basically OK? Will they be pressing for greater margins or higher prices? Will any of them go under?*
- *Will capacity for the product or service you buy be greater/less?*
- *Will your competitors (who are engaged in this Activity as well) seek to prevent your access to suppliers (by owning them for example)?*
- *Are there suppliers elsewhere in the world with whom it is feasible to deal?*

- *Are there substitute different products and services you could use?*
- *Might any of your suppliers become your competitors – might they integrate forward, in other words by acquisition or alliance? How serious would that be?*

Assessing supplier behaviour

- *How will each supplier develop/enhance the product or service you buy – where will they add value? How might you influence this?*
- *What might each do to raise switching costs so that it is more expensive for you to substitute? Can you influence that, do you want to?*
- *Is there potential for you to influence suppliers' strategies? Should you?*
- *What are the upsides and downsides of doing it?*

What you now have

The output of the six Activities you have been through will have provided you with a mass of information which will appear disorganized. Some of it will be duplicated, some irrelevant.

The probability, though, is that if you have allowed time, if you have 'consulted' (through group work) widely, if you have generated discussion and facilitated contribution, you will have all you need to paint a very accurate picture of the future competitive environment in which your organization and/or your unit will be operating.

Importantly, too, by the preamble supplied to each Activity, by the summaries of information at the end of each Activity you will have a *shared* sense of a future environment, and you will have taught your people a lot about the fundamentals of building strategy.

It now remains to translate this into first passes at strategic intent. Chapter 9 will do this for you.

There is no Help Screen for this chapter. The best recap of content is Figure 8.2, the competitive forces framework. If you use and understand this graphic, your thinking about the future will at least be directed and comprehensive.

9 Evaluating and clarifying strategic intent: our options for the future

Figure 9.1

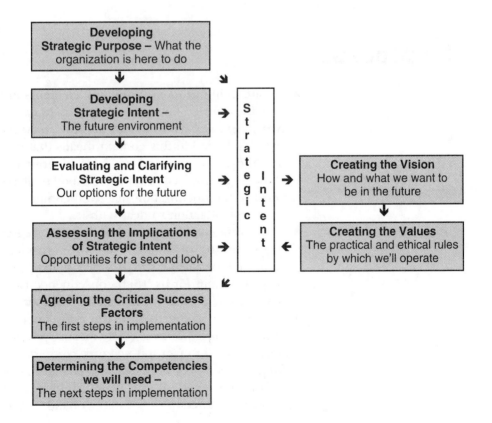

As Figure 9.1 indicates, we are moving, as promised, to using the data we generated in thinking about the future environment, and organizing it so that we can speculate on its relevance to our strategic intent, that is, deciding whether it will help us identify the major areas where we must concentrate our organizational energy to achieve our strategic purpose.

What this chapter should achieve

- It will pull together all the material we have generated in the last six Activities.
- It will give us a means of assessing the impact of the future environment on the organization or unit.
- It will again reveal the need for additional information.
- The output will be a first pass at strategic intent.

The process

- We are going to identify the key elements in all twelve Activities carried out thus far and accord each a score on two axes: the *likelihood* axis and the *consequence* axis. High likelihood in this context means that it is probable that the event or trend we have identified will occur. Obtaining agreement on the likelihood scale is important because the organization may well commit to a strategy or course of action to deal with it.
- The *consequence* scale measures the degree of consequence to, or impact on, the organization. Low consequence means that if/when it happens, it is not very important for us. High consequence means that if/when it happens, it is important for the organization.
- We are then going to split the consequence axis into *positive consequences* (that means positive for our organization or unit) and *negative consequences* – again from the perspective of our organization or unit.
- To do this exercise we need to have all the notes generated in Activities 8.1–8.6 to hand. If the Activities

have been conducted, as they optimally should have been, with several participants, we need them all.

- A good deal of the payoff from this Activity is the discussion it can generate among participants. In fact if it does not generate discussion and difference, you stand at risk of having compiled a business-as-usual future – this is unlikely, as we have seen.

First a word of explanation on the three axes we will be using.

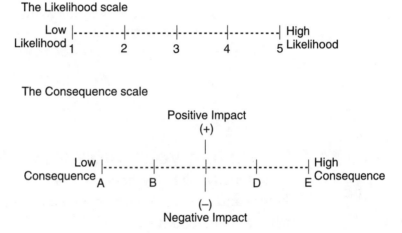

Figure 9.2
Likelihood and
consequence scales

Returning to the Magnum Motors case study in Chapter 8, the scores for two items of the motor car dealership's response to Activity 8.1 might be:

Item   **score:**

- Company car driver liable to heavier taxation – engine size.   5E(–)
- New marketing techniques emerging – highly targeted.   4B(+)

Explanation:

The likelihood of increased taxation is fairly certain. Because our dealership sells luxury cars, the consequence to us will be high, further the impact will be negative because taxation will drive car buyers to smaller vehicles.

New marketing techniques will almost certainly emerge; a 4 score. The consequence on us is fairly limited (B) because we are quite good at targeted database marketing now. The impact will be positive because, as a high-price supplier, our target customer is more visible and accessible.

Now let's proceed with the Activity of synthesizing the data you have generated.

9.1 Pulling your information together

This Activity probably benefits from somebody having done it before and then soliciting group discussion and feedback on the 'straw person' version.

The essence of the Activity is not 'to get it right' but to get agreement about the things which are really important. This is more likely to emerge from dialogue and discourse than from drafting.

1 ***Assemble all the responses*** *you have generated in the six previous Activities, i.e.:*

- *Determining the future*
- *Assessing the competition within the industry*
- *Assessing the new entrants*
- *Assessing changes in the product*
- *Assessing how customers or buyers will change*
- *Assessing how suppliers will change.*

2 *Set up five headings:*

- *The general environment*
- *The competitor environment (which includes existing players and new entrants)*
- *The future product*
- *The future buyer*
- *The future supplier.*

3 *Focus on each of the Activities in turn* *and:*

- *eliminate anything that you now think is trivial or ill advised*
- *combine things which are the same (sometimes you express the same idea in two different ways)*
- *compile a set of bullet point statements which cover the content of your Activity and the Activity of anyone else who is participating – again you will be combining here*
- *consider under which of the six headings the bullet point statement should feature – it can appear under more than one.*

4 *When you have compiled a list of bullets* **score each on the likelihood/consequence scale/impact scale.**

There follows an edited version of what the IT Department of Acme Corp. came up with.

Acme IT team

Figure 9.3

The general environment	Score
• There is a probability competitors will try to buy our company.	4E(−)
• The cost of the IT services will fall.	5E(+)
• The company will need more sophisticated IT services to keep abreast of competitors.	4E(+)
• IT services, though more sophisticated, will become more user friendly.	4D(0)
• IT services will need less maintenance.	2E(−)
• The company will be looking to us for increased efficiency and productivity – to improve overall company competitiveness.	4D(+)

The competitor environment	Score
• No other internal department in the co. will seek to provide the services we provide.	5E(+)
• External bureaus will proliferate, become less expensive and their response will be faster.	5E(−)
• If our company is sold a larger IT department could take over our function.	4E(−)
• The all-in cost of our unit could well induce the company to look at external sources for the services we provide.	4E(−)
• Our suppliers, hardware and software, may well become our competitors providing our company with the support we now provide.	3E(−)

The future product	Score
• The next phase of products needed by the company will be those integrating separate company functions – decision support products.	4E(+)
• Products needed will be software and network based.	5E(0)
• Generic rather than custom software will probably meet our needs.	4D(0)
• Hardware will need upgrading every 3–4 years.	3C(0)
• Potentially our most important product is consultancy and project management for the company.	5E(+)

The future buyer	Score
• Each functional department within our company is a potential buyer.	4E(+)
• Buyer criteria will be: minimal disruption, ease and transparency of operation, no downtime, integrity of data – making things easier for them.	5E(+)
• Buyers will be looking for advice and ideas – we will become their source of expertise.	5E(+)
• If we are bought, our future buyer is an unknown quantity; we need to develop competencies which are valued in a broader corporate environment where we would be competing with other depts.	3E(0)

Figure 9.3
Continued

The future supplier	Score
● Manufacturers of hardware and software are likely to 'integrate forward', i.e. provide the support we now provide.	3E(−)
● The market of which we are a part will continue to be served by a number of hardware and software suppliers (little chance of monopolies).	4E(+)
● For some key manufacturers (e.g. SAP) we may not be a large enough customer to get high levels of support from them.	4D(−)

A few notes on this example:

Developing a strategy for an internal company unit is really no different from developing one for a complete company. The scope of strategic intent is likely to be more limited because it must fit within the overall parameters of the organization of which the unit is a part.

Sometimes, as in this case, the competitive environment is a lot clearer in a unit than it would be for a whole company, but it is interesting that this unit perceives itself to be under potential competitive threat from its suppliers, from unspecified sources in the event of an ownership change and, because of their cost base, from bureaus as well.

In the event, as we shall see, synthesizing all the data they had generated in the purpose and competitive analysis phases led the unit to a reappraisal of their purpose, and a clear consensus among unit members and others within the company as to strategic intent.

Implications of your scoring on the consequence/likelihood scale

We now need to assess your evaluation of the key issues you have identified. This is what your scoring implies. You will find it is a bit more complex than usual because you are dealing with three axes: consequence, likelihood and positive/negative impact.

Figure 9.4

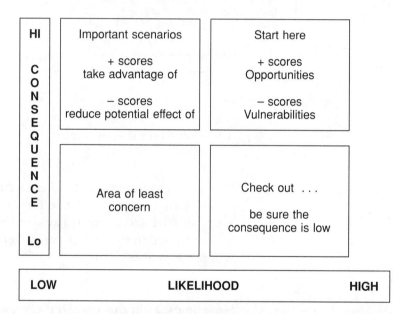

High likelihood 4 and 5, high consequence D and E scores are those you will want to look at first:

- If these scores are positive, i.e. (+), they are *opportunities* which should be turned into positive advantages for the unit or organization
- If these scores are negative, i.e. (–), they are *vulnerabilities* or weakness which should be addressed to turnaround, to cure or to develop some strategy of avoidance.

Low likelihood 1 and 2, high consequence D and E should be looked at as potential scenarios and you should consider some action planning as to what you might do in the event of them happening to:

- take advantage of *positive* (+) ratings
- mitigate or seek to reduce the potential effect of *negative* (-) ratings.

High likelihood 4 and 5, low consequence A and B are scores you should also take a look at to be certain the consequence is low. If the likelihood is high, the probability is that the event or scenario is imminent. If that is the case, be sure the unit is unaffected or minimally affected.

Low likelihood 1 and 2, low consequence A and B should be looked at as potential future

- advantages if they are positive (+)
- concerns if they are negative (-).

The rationale for doing this, even if the likelihood seems low, is that they were none the less important enough for you or the group to have identified so they are probably not dismissable even though they may not be imminent.

What conclusions? Your strategic intent is emerging

It is difficult to provide a structured framework for the next Activity. Essentially the purpose is to conclude, from the priorities you have identified, a series of strategic intentions which, you will remember, collectively become a statement of the unit's strategic intent. Follow the tips in the Activity but be guided more by what you need to get out of it rather than the processes suggested.

The case study for Acme which follows, and that for Magnum later in the chapter, both use the same format, and you might find their examples helpful.

9.2 Drawing conclusions from information

First, do a mind shift from thinking about the five headings under which you compiled key statements to thinking about the priorities you have assigned each.

Secondly, read the purpose statement you prepared beforehand and keep it to hand.

1 *Identify the opportunities and vulnerabilities – the high scores which would fall in the top-right box – and take a careful look:*

- *first at all the positives – the opportunities*
- *next at all the negatives – the vulnerabilities.*

Reflect on what they are telling you.

2 *A series of underlying requirements will start to become clear. These requirements will signal things which the unit is going to have to deal with in the environment you have envisaged. Being able to express the requirement is the precursor to being able to declare an intention – a **strategic intention**.*

You will find that requirement/intention strands surface relatively easily, and you will find that they are not unexpected. They usually confirm your views, though you might be surprised by the effect of the consequence/likelihood/impact scale.

3 *Try to express each in the briefest possible way, a headline and bulleted definers is a good way (see examples which follow). Resist the urge to express these requirements/intentions as objectives; resist the urge to be too definitive or prescriptive. Absolutely resist the urge to start describing how to deal with each. We are interested in **what must be done**, not how to do it.*

4 *As each requirement/intention becomes clear, trawl through your other statements (no matter how you have scored them) to see if any others match or are the same things surfacing in a different guise. Combine where you can, but do not force fit or lose definition.*

5 *Do the above, moving progressively down the priority scale until you feel you have established a realistic and viable set of requirements and intentions – things which your head and heart tell you are the right things to be focusing on given the analysis you have undertaken.*

6 *Stop when you think that you have covered everything you believe needs to be achieved. Tell yourself that you are going to have to live with these decisions for years.*

Here is an edited version of the first pass that the Acme IT department got out of their exercise. This is the outcome of a strategy workshop to which participants came after their separate responses to Activity 9.2 had been collated and merged. The first part of this workshop was spent in agreeing and amending the statements made in the various Activities. In the case below, we have called these the underlying statements. The second part of the workshop generated the responses shown in the example below.

Read the left-hand column, the underlying statements first. This shows how Acme IT have grouped their thinking. In the event the bulk of the strategy workshop was spent in discussing the implications which support the emerging strategic intentions.

Acme IT team

Figure 9.5

Underlying statements	Implications	Emerging strategic intention
• There is a probability competitors will try to buy our company. • If our company is sold a larger IT department could take over our function. • If we are bought, our future buyer is an unknown quantity; we need to develop competencies which are valued in a broader corporate environment where we could be competing with other departments. • The all-in cost of our unit could well induce the company to look at external sources for the services we provide. • The company will be looking to us for increased efficiency and productivity – to improve overall company competitiveness.	As an operating unit we are vulnerable because of: • the perceived probability of our company being bought • the fact that we do not provide a service which adds value others could not add • we are either actually or potentially more expensive than external providers might be.	**We need to increase our importance to the company:** • Contribute in a different way, provide services which contribute more towards strategy (i.e. long term) rather than at the operational level we now focus on. • We must add unique value. • We must be able to survive in the more competitive world which would exist internally after we are bought. **We need to provide the company with better value for money:** • Reduce our establishment cost. • Possibly earn money by consulting externally.

Underlying statements	Implications	Emerging strategic intention
• The company will need more sophisticated IT services to keep abreast of competitors. • Products needed will be software and network based. • Generic rather than custom software will probably meet our needs. • The next phase of products needed by the company will be those integrating separate company functions. • Each functional department within our company is a potential buyer. • Hardware will need upgrading every 3–4 years. • Buyer criteria will be: minimal disruption, ease and transparency of operation, no downtime, integrity of data, making things easier for them. • Buyers will be looking for advice and ideas – we will become their source of expertise.	We think that we have a fairly clear idea about the future product needs for the company . . . but . . . we actually are not certain whether this vision is the way the company sees it. We have no idea what the greater integration of company functions implies for the company. If we are right about networks and functional integration the relatively lower priority we have given to hardware upgrades is likely to be wrong. In general we are proceeding with a set of assumptions which need to be tested; they cannot be tested simply by asking around – we need to develop an entire IT strategy for the company and then to sell it in.	**We need to develop a strategic plan for the use of IT within the company:** • long term • based on enabling the company to achieve competitive advantage • implications thoroughly assessed and spelt out • we must co-ordinate. **We need to redefine our relationship to the organization:** • Position ourselves as consultants rather than implementers of new programmes and troubleshooters. • Actively seek internal customer input rather than making the assumption that our simplistic criteria are valid. • Initiate a programme of feedback and information to customers. **We need to develop the skill sets to support this role:** • Better external benchmark information. • Better expertise on supplier developments.

Underlying statements	Implications	Emerging strategic intention
• The cost of IT services will fall. • IT services, though more sophisticated, will become more user friendly • IT services will need less maintenance. • External bureaus will proliferate, become less expensive and their response will be faster. • Our suppliers, hardware and software, may well become our competitors, providing our company with the support we now provide. • Manufacturers of hardware and software are likely to 'integrate forward', i.e. provide the sort of support we now provide. • For some key manufacturers (e.g. SAP) we may not be a large enough customer to get a high level of support from them.	Looking at bureaus and suppliers as potential threats or competitors is a mistake, rather we should be transferring some of the routine installation and maintenance work we now do for them thus freeing us up for a higher value added role. Good relationships with suppliers becomes very important because they are the people who can help us upgrade our skills sets and competencies. If we embrace rather than compete with suppliers and bureaus, we will need to become expert negotiators – a further skill set need. The better our relationships and breadth of contacts with suppliers or bureaus, the better we will be able to shop and buy on behalf of the company.	**Cultivate partnering relationships with suppliers:** • Improve our knowledge of external development. • Facilitate benchmarking. • Squeeze added value out of them. **Outsource or seek external bureau provision for defined internal functions:** • System maintenance. • Web site creation and maintenance. • Troubleshooting.

After some more polishing Acme Corp.'s IT department was able to make a statement of strategic intent which, though still not perfect, certainly provided them with a foundation on which they could proceed. They were excited, however, to have established a new purpose for themselves which the participants all felt added valuable depth and context to their jobs.

This is what it looked like:

Purpose

To provide a cost-effective means of Acme Corp. achieving competitive advantage through information technology and supporting systems

---

Strategic intent

Intention 1   To position ourselves as a credible IT and systems consultancy resource with all functional departments.

Intention 2   To assure continuity of IT installation, training, maintenance and troubleshooting; making IT easier for all employees (i.e. the scope of our present activity).

Intention 3   To develop a strategic plan for IT systems to serve the company through 2002.

Intention 4   To reduce our cost base.

Intention 5   To upskill the intellectual base of the department so that its competency is equal to the demands of Intention 1.

Intention 6   To manage our relationships/alliances with bureaus, software and hardware suppliers which enable us to learn from them, buy intelligently from them, and achieve the maximum added value from them.

The inevitable assertion after reading the examples we have used is: 'well it's perfectly obvious what the IT department should be doing. It certainly does not need all that analysis to be able to make the Purpose and Statements of Strategic Intent.'

Experience has led me to challenge this response because:

- Very few functional departments are capable of making such statements in the context of their overall relationship to the organizations in which they operate.
- Even fewer are guided on a day-to-day basis by the clarity of purpose and strategy that such an exercise provides.
- Even fewer have the level of internal alignment and support for the strategy among their people that the process of developing that strategy will have engendered.
- Where a strategy development exercise has taken place and is actually guiding the behaviour and prioritizing of the department, a higher degree of employee satisfaction certainly exists.

Among the more usual reactions to this 'first-tangible-fruits' stage of strategy development are:

- 'We *should* have been able to make those statements right at the outset.'
- A brief sense of self-satisfaction which is inevitably superseded by disappointment that nothing more radical has emerged.
- There is often a sense of gloom at how much we are going to have to change.

Because the transition from generating information to crafting a strategic intent is so critical in developing a strategy, it probably helps if we also look at another example from the perspective of an organization rather than an operating unit. We return to the up-market motorcar dealership, Magnum Motors.

To get some perspective we will backtrack to look at the results they developed from the Competitive Forces Activities.

Magnum Motors

Figure 9.6

The general environment	Score
• The big car will be discriminated against making it more expensive to buy, run, tax and insure.	5D(−)
• The economy will deteriorate between 2000 and 2003.	4E(−)
• The market will shrink or, at best, remain static in unit terms for 4–5 years.	5E(−)
• Less money will be made on service (longer service intervals).	3E(−)
• Our owners are seeking improved profitability.	5E(−)
• Investment cash for the business will be hard to find.	5D(−)

The competitor environment	Score
• Few if any of our known competitors will go under – they will 'tough it out' as we intend to.	4D(−)
• Price wars are probable despite slim margins.	3C(−)
• The manufacturer will enter the direct supply market more aggressively.	3E(−)
• Possibility of large retailers, e.g. supermarkets with large sites adding new or used car lots – the TESCO car?	2B(−)
• Unlikely that the manufacturer will appoint more franchisees in our area of potential influence.	4C(+)

The future product	Score
• The manufacturer will extend the product range down market.	5C(0)
• More technologically advanced – more reliable, longer service intervals.	4C(+)
• Will require highly skilled service engineers.	4D(−)
• Will be more environmentally friendly but still attract criticism.	4C(+)

The future buyer	Score
• Corporate buyers will squeeze us harder – we will have to add more value.	5D(−)
• A new and largely unknown buyer for the lower end of the market range.	5E(0)
• Will have high expectations of service, reliability, and all interactions with the dealership.	5C(+)

Figure 9.6
Continued

The future supplier	Score
• Manufacturer likely to shave margins and find ways of recovering income from dealerships.	4D(−)
• Manufacturer likely to become a competitor supplier.	4D(−)
• Manufacturer likely to be more demanding of dealership performance to retain franchise.	4C(0)
• Investor (supplier of money) likely to be harder to find, require higher ROI.	4E(−)
• Labour market (supplier of staff) harder to find good white-collar workers . . .	4D(−)
• . . . easier to find engineers/ technicians.	4D(+)

A few notes are required on these two case studies. The two big differences between Magnum and the Acme IT team are:

1 Magnum is answerable to investors who, as we know, are also line managers in the organization. This coupled with Magnum's wish to grow the business puts investment and return on investment centre stage for them. Ultimately they are looking for increased shareholder value, not dividends. The external investor who holds 50 per cent of the company, however, is looking for both increase in shareholder value and dividends.
2 Magnum is tied by its franchise to the manufacturer. The manufacturer is, of course, a supplier, but a supplier of critical importance having some of the properties of an owner. The upside of this is that the manufacturer's probable strategy is known. The downside is that the manufacturer's behaviour is life or death for Magnum.

If we now look at how Magnum translated its assessment into the front end of strategic intention, we see an example of an organization, as distinct from an operating department, developing its strategy.

	Underlying statements	Implications	Emerging strategic intent
Figure 9.7	• The big car will be discriminated against making it more expensive to buy, run, tax and insure. • The economy will deteriorate between 2000 and 2003. • The market will shrink or, at best, remain static in unit terms for 4–5 years. • Few if any of our known competitors will go under – they will tough it out as we intend to. • The buyer will have higher expectations of service reliability and all interactions with the dealership.	Our prime market – large, luxury, upmarket, well-engineered cars – is likely to shrink and get tougher. We could aggressively pursue a larger share of a shrinking market through targeted marketing and discounting. This looks like high risk and our gut sense is that we would not be able to meet our growth ambitions for the company in this market because to do so would cost too much. On the other hand we want to stay in the market because when it is good (after 2003) it is very, very good. We also want to maintain our long-term relationship with the manufacturer and our servicing skills.	**We will maintain our share of our prime market. This means:** • we must improve the efficiency of our targeted marketing • we can confront a decrease in margin, but we are not prepared to lose money to maintain our share. **We must find ways of adding increased value for the individual level customer and for the corporate buyer:** • Taking a new approach to customer satisfaction – *really knowing* what they want, need, value and *really supplying* it. • If we are to minimize the effects of price war we can only do it through customer satisfaction.

EVALUATING AND CLARIFYING STRATEGIC INTENT: OUR OPTIONS FOR THE FUTURE

Figure 9.7 Continued	Underlying statements	Implications	Emerging strategic intention
	• The manufacturer will extend the product range down market. • A new and largely unknown buyer for the lower end of the market range which the manufacturer is adding. • Investor (supplier of money) likely to be harder to find and to require higher ROI. • Investment cash for the business will be hard to find. • Our owners will be seeking improved profitability.	We need to develop a second business addressed to another lower-priced market sector. This should really be the main vehicle for growth while the up-market business is flat. We cannot do this on our present site because there is no room and because we could not water down our up-market image with cheaper cars. If we were in a lower-priced market as well, the manufacturer would see us as more valuable because we would support its whole range. This lower-priced business would be less capital intensive – + ROI. It should also be more profitable because it would benefit from economies made possible because of the existence of the up-market business.	**We need to build or acquire a second business selling a lower-priced product to a different market:** • This new business will be at below £15,000 unit price; the £9,999.99 market. • We need to design the business so that it benefits from maximum synergy with the existing business. • We need to involve our prime investor in this strategy – and we need to identify (an)other potential investor(s).

Figure 9.7
Continued

Underlying statements	Implications	Emerging strategic intention
• The manufacturer will enter the direct supply market. • Unlikely that the manufacturer will appoint more franchisees in our area of potential influence. • Manufacturer likely to shave margins and find ways of recovering income from dealerships. • Manufacturer likely to be more demanding of dealership performance to retain franchise.	At the end of the line we must assure continued good relations with the manufacturer. We would like to be more powerful in influencing how the manufacturer behaves, particularly in the areas of terms of business with dealerships and in their general approach to the market – awarding franchises etc. It would be good if we had more clout, but if the manufacturer thought we were out of line it would be damaging.	**We need to develop a discreet pressure group with other franchisees in the area so that we can speak to the manufacturer with one voice on key issues:** • Strike a careful balance as to what aspects we organize around – select a few key things material to our common businesses. • Avoid confrontation with the manufacturer but keep up the pressure. • Sup with a long spoon!

Working from this discussion, Magnum predicated the following:

Strategic intent

Intention 1 We will seek to maintain our share of the up-market car business rather than expand it for the foreseeable future. We anticipate an upturn in the market about 2003 at which time we wish to be well placed to take advantage of the inherent profitability of this market's reflation.

Intention 2 We intend to build new, improved levels of customer satisfaction so that we are literally the best in the business achieving higher levels of CSI than all our competitors.

Intention 3 We enter the £9,999.99 priced market through acquisition, or by setting up a new venture. This venture will be independent of the existing business but the combined cost bases of the two businesses are to be lower than each would be individually. We are looking to revenue growth, higher ROI, and improved overall profitability as a result.

Intention 4 We intend to establish a user group of manufacturer dealerships in the area to interact productively and collectively with the manufacturer.

10 Creating the vision and creating the values

Figure 10.1

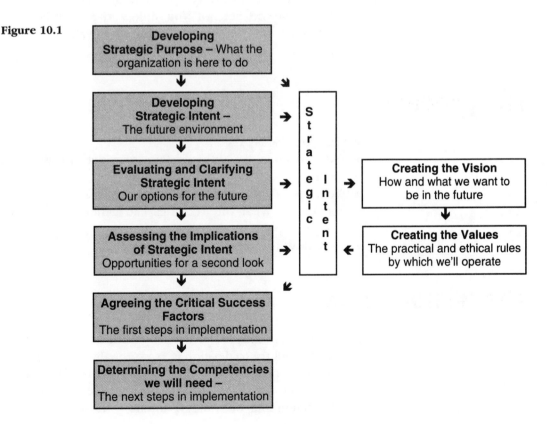

This chapter leads us into the more 'touchy feely' areas of strategy development. The predominant view among strategists is that the whole exercise should start with getting clear about the vision. My own view is that the appropriate place in the development process is now, right after we have developed the first pass at the strategic intent. It seems to me that at this point we have drawn a good picture of how we will address the future. It is the right time to ask the question: 'If that is what we think we should do, what could we become, what might we able to achieve, how would we like to feel about ourselves when we get there?'

What this chapter should achieve

- You should end up with an understanding of why vision and values are important; just what purpose they serve in an organization's or unit's strategy and in the way people operate as a result.
- You will have a couple of options of exercises to use with your own people to develop vision and values.
- You should be able, if you follow the exercises, to develop a useful vision and a viable set of values for your organization or unit.

The process

- First we discuss vision.
- Two versions of Activities are provided to develop vision.
- We look at the output of our two cases, to help understand what the Activities can generate and how groups respond.
- We follow the same process with values.

The 'vision thing'

Strategic vision, in the sense we will be using it and in the way in which we will try to develop it, is essentially an attempt to get agreement about a destination: where we are going; what it might be like once we get there. In that we already have some understanding of strategic intent - those battlefields where we will compete, those areas where we intend to put our greatest efforts – we need to close the circle by obtaining agreement about what that destination might look like. We need, in short, to add qualitative and aspirational ingredients to the good, hard thinking we have done so far.

It has became fashionable to be derisory about the concept of vision. Indications are, however, that where organizations or operating units have had a powerful sense of vision, they have performed spectacularly well. Vision provides a pull for the organization, a commonality of purpose about what we would like to become. Again, to return to a repetitive theme, if the members of the organization or unit are involved in developing the vision, the experience is powerful and the effect of the exercise is always positive. Put in the negative, a vision which has not been contributed to by key participants will need to be sold to them with the attendant risk that they may or may not buy it.

Looking at vision after a first pass at strategic intent helps add a qualitatively different ingredient to the strategy. What we have talked about so far is how we might survive and prosper in a competitive environment. As we move to vision (and values) we start to deal with ideas of personal fulfilment, pride in participation, the pursuit of something worth while. In some ways we could look at the strategic intent as a base camp from which we might attempt the assault on the peak.

key concept

The danger is that the aspirational element in vision-building exercises deteriorates into the worst examples of the old-fashioned mission statement: 'to be the biggest . . ., the most profitable . . ., provide the best quality . . . ' and all that good stuff which sends the staff into a fit of yawning.

One of the ways out of this that I have found is to split out vision and values. Combining them produces the anodyne, unexceptionable mission statement which by and large does not pull, nor does it push, it does not even nudge.

Separating them strikes a balance between aspiration and ethics, and allows focus on each.

It is interesting that when we think of a future, what we would like to become, we use a word like 'vision' which concentrates specifically on one sense, the visual sense. The reason for this is that people find it easier to create images of what things will be like in the future and so in developing strategic vision we rely on visualizing the way we want to be. It also produces better insight if we use some of the techniques of creativity sessions. In the Activity which follows we use analogies to help the process of visualization. Let us see if this approach works for you.

10.1 Developing a vision

Step 1   *Assemble your group. Be sure that all the main members of the unit or, if an organization, the major functional or divisional heads are present.*

Step 2   *Position this (probably 3–4 hour exercise) as an opportunity for some fun, for some creativity, and some dreaming. Make sure that everybody realizes there is a serious intent to the Activity even if the atmosphere is relatively light-hearted.*

Step 3   *Be clear about what we intend to get out of this Activity. It is:*

An agreed vision of what we would like the unit or organization to be like in the future. A set of statements or descriptors which give us something to reach for, something to aspire to.

Make the point about a vision being, unsurprisingly, visual even if we have to express it in words.

Step 4   *Divide the group into syndicates of four to six people each. Label the syndicates; the Animal group, the Motor Car group, the Building group etc.*

Invite each group to select an example (animal, motor car or building) which is most typical of the unit or organization as it is today. Tell them that each group will have to explain their choice; why did they select the example they did. What characteristics of their example are similar to the way the organization is today.

Allow them thirty minutes or so to reach agreement and develop their case.

Step 5 *Now invite each group to select an example of how they would like the unit or organization to be in the future – say in five years' time. Tell them that each group will have to explain their choice; why did they select the example they did. What characteristics of their example are similar to the way they would like the organization to be in the future.*

Allow them thirty minutes or so to reach agreement and develop their case.

Step 6 *Take feedback from each group, and as it is going on seek those commonalities which will have been expressed in each analogy. As each piece of feedback is completed summarize the main characteristics you thought the group had identified now and in the future and invite them, and the larger group, to comment and enhance the descriptions.*

Record main characteristics on a flip chart if possible.

Step 7 *Regroup the syndicates mixing participants differently. Take one or more of the characteristics which have been identified as desirable in a future context and allocate them to a syndicate – two or three characteristics per syndicate works well.*

Invite the syndicate to translate the characteristics developed in the analogies into descriptors of what they would actually look like in the unit or organization in the future.

Step 8   *Take feedback and open for shared discussion and input.*
Summarize as best you can and gain agreement.

Step 9   *Write up the results later, circulate to all participants and seek their*
input and alterations so that an agreed report can be tabled.

Note:

1 If the group is relatively small you can work with one of the three classes of analogies, animals or cars or buildings rather than all three. Working in syndicates, though, is very important as the small group activity tends to allow people to build imaginatively on each others' thinking.

2 Some facilitators do the same exercise with pictures, and it works well too. You will need to provide an eclectic selection of fifty to a hundred pictures of three broad kinds:

   (a) Pictures which are in tune with the unit's or organization's activities but do not necessarily reflect what actually happens – sports pictures might be added to the animal, building, car lists above. Aerial pictures, maps, plants and vegetation are all good candidates.

   (b) A second category of pictures should have emotional content: courage, happiness, stability, security, winning, challenge, defeat, grief, and so on.

   (c) You should also look for pictures using bright colours, abstracts, patterns, and so on.

3 You will find that it is quite easy to assemble a group of pictures that are suitable and usable for the Activity: photographs, postcards, cartoons, art work, great masters are all good candidates.

4 If you use this approach, spread the pictures out on table tops. After positioning the Activity as above, invite participants to wander round and select three or four pictures at random; this must happen in silence. Pictures are then taken back to the syndicate and, again without speaking, participants group the pictures they have chosen in relationship to each other so that the members of the syndicate are satisfied. The group is then allowed to speak to each other and should explore the implications of the messages they have developed for themselves.

5 I have found that if you use the picture approach it is better not to ask the syndicates to assemble a set of pictures typical of the way the organization or unit is now; you are better

advised to focus the entire exercise of the future – the way we would like it to be.

By way of an example, let us see how our friends at the IT department at Acme managed this Activity. The whole department took part as did the director of Acme to whom the IT Manager reports. In their case, they chose to handle only animals and buildings. Here (warts and all) is the record of their session.

Acme IT team

Syndicate 1 – the animals
Animal analogy – the way we are now:

Squirrel because
- we're active all the time; constantly running about
- we're ingenious, clever at solving problems on a one-time basis
- we're inefficient – we don't remember where we hid the nuts, i.e. we are not documenting properly to enshrine and retrieve best practice
- sometimes we perform amazing athletic feats; people are astonished when we recover what look like disastrous situations (mainly loss of data)
- we are 'cute' – we are liked but we are not taken seriously in the context of the business
- sometimes we're considered vermin, accused of environmental damage – when the system crashes
- we increase in number every year – departmental cost!

Animal we'd like to be in the future:

Gorilla because
- we'd be taken seriously – big and hairy rather than small and furry
- we'd be among the most intelligent of the animals in the forest
- we would be creating and operating in an environment which we carefully controlled and policed (the social system of a troop of gorillas)
- we'd be operating as a team – defined roles; specific capabilities
- we'd be better than other animals at using rudimentary tools (outside vendors, service bureaus etc.)
- we would have fewer, if any, predators (potential corporate usurpers of our function)

- if we got into a fight we'd probably win, but we would not get into many fights because we'd be too scary to mess with.

Syndicate 2 – the buildings

This syndicate originally chose to use car analogies, but they found it too constraining and opted to change to buildings.

Building – the way we are now:

This is a school building, originally a small brick core with classrooms, some offices and an assembly hall. As time has gone on the school has been under pressure to expand. Things have been added to the building – some new buildings which are out of keeping with the original, some Portakabins were installed on a 'temporary basis' twenty years ago, and they are still there:

- we keep 'making do' rather than clearing the site and rebuilding
- everything is a bit dilapidated and in need of renewal
- it is all so inefficient that it costs a lot to run
- the building is not contributing to the kids' education – it is making it more difficult for them
- we are constantly repairing the fabric, distracting us from the real task of teaching the kids
- we never really know where the next problem will arise
- we are not using the site properly – we are still having to add more and add it faster.

The building we'd like to be is the *Millennium Dome*:

- love it or hate it you know why it's there, and what it is there for
- it is large and flexible and can accommodate a wide variety of applications
- it is served by an excellent infrastructure (trains, car parks and so on)
- it is (likely to be) pretty efficient
- given the space it covers and multiple services it can accommodate, it is pretty cheap to build
- it will attract a lot of customers
- people will look back on it and say that it was all worth it
- people take it seriously and remember it.

Note: Also like the Millennium Dome our IT department is often considered a waste of money which could have been more effectively deployed elsewhere in the business.

Acme IT department translated their vision into a set of statements as follows:

- We will be viewed as an authoritative, solid and highly competent resource to the organization.
- Our approach will be seen as strategic, focused, enshrining best practice, and supporting and enabling the organization's broader strategic intent.
- We will be seen as having provided really good value for the money we cost the organization.
- We will feel secure because we are so good at what we do and acknowledged to be so.
- We will attract customers because we are regarded as flexible and accommodating to their needs and views.
- One of the keys to our success will be our ability to operate as a team.

The millennium gorilla, the King Kong of IT.

It is often the case, and I think this is true for Acme's IT department, that the final version of the vision seems a bit watery and anodyne. The value of the exercise really consists of the following:

- The Activity has caused participants to reflect on what they do, how they do it in a way which is likely to be different from the way they normally discuss the business – new perspectives will have opened, new insights gained.
- The fact that *all* members of the department experience the Activity creates a shared responsibility for the outcome; a certain bonding between members develops as a result of the mutuality of experience – a great team-building exercise incidentally.
- Part of the strategy-building process is to 'tumble the business' so that a different facet is revealed by each Activity. This generally provides insights and enriches peoples' understanding and responsibility.
- The department now has a common vocabulary, a shared shorthand, 'the millennium gorilla', which has a specific and precise meaning for all of them.

In truth it is often through the process of strategy-building rather than by the outcome that the value is delivered to the organization.

Creating the values

Among the most powerful experiences a unit leader or a chief executive can undertake with his or her immediate reports is a values-building exercise. It is rare that those who have participated leave such an exercise unaffected, most find that it significantly enhances their understanding of their job and their appreciation of the organization. People frequently find that the insights it offers into the motivation of their boss and of their colleagues provides valuable clues as to how to deal with them in the future as well.

Determining the values of the organization or the unit is about reaching agreement on the practical and ethical rules by which we will operate. It is a code of behaviour which affects the way one does one's job. We want to establish those things which the organization encourages, supports, allows or countenances; we equally want to identify, usually only by implication, those things which are not allowed, which are frowned upon and which might attract sanctions if the employee committed them.

Many organizations are pursuing policies of empowerment. That means allowing people at relatively lower levels in the pecking order to take decisions which commit the organization. Empowering your people certainly implies that you establish and agree the boundaries of any employee's latitude for decision-making, but potentially more important is the contribution of a well-articulated and agreed set of values. These help and guide the thinking employee and provide a context for decisions. Agreed values also provide the employee with a reasonable level of assurance that decisions he or she takes will be supported.

Values also determine what is called the 'culture' of the organization. That is the set of commonly held beliefs of what goes and what does not go in this organization or unit. Culture identifies the sort of behaviour which is encouraged and rewarded, the sort that gets overlooked or ignored and the sort that gets punished.

Values must be distinguished from the procedures of the company. They are also different from the rules outlined in contracts of employment or in any disciplinary procedures which may be operating in the organization, and hence the unit. Procedures and rules are black and white and should be relatively unambiguous in their requirement. Values click in where the rules run out.

Values are deeply committing for the organization. If time and risk is to be taken to determine values, they must be lived by, be seen to be lived by, and people must, regardless of seniority or rank within the organization, be capable of being held to account for breaching them.

The evidence is that any group of employees distils most of its understanding of values by observing the behaviour of their immediate boss. Most of the rest of their understanding is derived from observing colleagues' behaviour and the boss's reaction to that behaviour. Note that the word used is 'behaviour'; in other words it is not what the boss and colleagues *say* that determines values, it is what they *do*!

Try the following Activity to conduct a values-building exercise.

10.2 Creating the values

A facilitated group environment with lots of opportunity for discussion and input from all members is emphatically the best way to conduct this Activity. If yours is a unit, see if you can involve all members. If the unit is large, conduct the Activity more than once feeding back to each group the outputs of the previous groups.

If you are conducting this on behalf of an organization you should plan to involve everybody in the organization in it at some time or another as outlined above. Simply handing out a set of values in the formulation and discussion of which employees have not participated is likely to be greeted with indifference at least, cynicism at worst.

Step 1   *Explain the purpose of the meeting:*

To agree a set of values by which we will operate and conduct ourselves and the activities of our unit/organization.

Explain what you know about how values work and why they are important.
Explain how declaring a set of values is deeply committing for participants and for their colleagues. Make clear that they too will be committed by the outcome of the session.
Suggest that they might think it is funny to espouse silly values in the exercises, at the end of the line, however, great organizations are rarely seen as cynical and opportunistic.

Step 2   *Form syndicates and have them work first individually, then collectively on the items below:*

(a) List the quality criteria (the hard issues) your customers should expect of the product or service the unit/organization provides.
(b) Complete the following statement (as many times as you feel important):

As a customer of this unit/organization it is good to deal with them because, besides meeting their quality criteria they (here add the soft issues) _____

Have the syndicates report back and initiate a discussion in which you seek clarification, justification and pragmatic reality. Let the group drive their definitions and argue their corner. Record outcomes and agreements on a flip chart.

Step 3   *Have the syndicates work on the following items.*
Complete the following statements as many times as you think necessary:

(a) As a supplier to this unit/organization I have always found them to be _____

(b) As the auditors/controller of this unit/organization I have always found them to be _____

Have the syndicates report back and initiate a discussion in which you seek clarification, justification and pragmatism. Let the group drive their definitions and argue their corner. Record outcomes and agreements on a flip chart.

Step 4   *Have the syndicates work on the following item.*

Complete the following statement as many times as needed:

(a) I am pleased to be the owner of this organization (director in charge of this unit) because _____
_____

Have the syndicates report back and initiate a discussion in which you seek clarification, justification and pragmatism. Let the group drive their definitions and argue their corner. Record outcomes and agreements on a flip chart.

Step 5   *Next have the syndicates work on the following item.*

Complete the following statement as many times as needed:

(a) As an employee of this organization and work unit I value working here because _____
_____

Have the syndicates report back and initiate a discussion in which you seek clarification, justification and pragmatism. Let the group drive their definitions and argue their corner. Record outcomes and agreements on a flip chart.

Step 6   *Before the group disperses summarize orally the contents of the flip charts and invite any additions, further comments etc.*

Suggest that the same values may have emerged under different guises and perhaps expressed slightly differently to fit the particular application.

Tell them that you will, with one or two others they nominate, rework the contents of the flip chart pages into a set of values which you will circulate for their consideration. They will be able to use this opportunity to add, editorialize, correct or whatever they think appropriate.

Step 7   *Draft an editorially acceptable version of the flip charts and circulate once inviting amendments and once in final format.*

Let us see how our friends in the Acme IT team managed the Activity. This is the third draft of the document which was distilled from Activity 10.2. Incidentally it was during this exercise that the team first became aware of kaizen (see below). They found the principles very appropriate to their need, but as a functional department they felt they could adopt kaizen only in the way they ran their team. Since the exercise the idea of kaizen has percolated further through Acme and is achieving some success.

Acme IT team's values exercise

The Acme IT team charter

Our commitment to quality and service
Our definition of quality will exceed 'fitness for purpose'. Our first responsibility will be to meet customer criteria but we have a further ethical responsibility to educate our customer to consider best-in-class criteria and to be ready to meet these.

Our commitment to customer relations
We believe that the value added by the individual interacting with the customer is, after quality and service (see above), the key component in satisfying our customer. Each member of the team takes individual responsibility for consistently adding that value.

Our commitment to Acme
The IT team exists to provide Acme with competitive advantage through IT and systems. It is our responsibility to:

- assure our activities and operations are consistent with Acme's strategic direction
- assure through education and dissemination of information at all levels that the organization is aware of leading-edge and world-class IT applications so that it can make appropriate strategic choices
- operate at levels of expense which provide the organization with best-in-class value for money.

Our commitment to suppliers
We will provide the best quality of qualitative and quantitative information to suppliers to assure that, without prejudice, each is fully aware of our needs and expectations.

We will expect suppliers to respect strict rules of confidentiality, and we will reciprocate that undertaking.

We expect and will make clear that we look to our suppliers as a major source of learning and education and that this criterion could influence our selection of suppliers.

Our commitment to our people
We want to adopt the ten principles of kaizen:

- Focus on customers.
- Make improvements unceasingly.
- Acknowledge problems openly.
- Promote openness.
- Work as a team.
- Manage projects cross-functionally.
- Nurture supportive relationships.
- Develop self-discipline.
- Inform every employee.
- Enable every employee.

We want also to promote the whole idea of personal learning and professional development in the team and our commitment here is that through appraisal systems we will seek to facilitate personal, professional and career development.

Magnum took the values exercise very seriously. They are sensitive to the poor ethical reputation which car dealerships frequently have. Even though they are a very up-market organization they believe that sharp practice is often unfairly attributed to them particularly in their used car sales department. Their clients frequently joke with them about 'clocked milometers' and so on.

Another problem Magnum has is that because the luxury car they sell is very much a status symbol, and because the dealership is located in a 'mixed' socioeconomic area, they often make sales to customers who arrive with a carrier bag full of money. Magnum is never too sure about how to deal with this sort of customer.

Magnum's code of conduct

Magnum values its relationships with its customers as one of the prime assets of its business. It seeks to exceed customer expectation in all interactions with customers and to build long-term lasting and trusting relationships. It is the responsibility of each member of staff to help deliver these levels of customer satisfaction.

Magnum acknowledges the potential for unethical practice in the used car business. There are no circumstances under which the company can afford to be party to such practices. For the avoidance of doubt, Magnum regards any breach of this value as grounds for disciplinary procedures.

Magnum provides a premium product in all three of its major areas of activity; new vehicle sales, used car sales and vehicle servicing. It is a requirement that such premium products and services are delivered fault free, spotlessly clean and in peak working order without exception. It is the responsibility of each member of staff to support and sustain this requirement.

In its relationships with [the manufacturer] Magnum intends to continue to be seen as the flagship dealer in every respect except size. Exceeding the performance of our competitors is an ongoing expectation, and being the best in class is a continuing aspiration.

Magnum offers its employees good working conditions, competitive rates of pay, and the opportunity to learn and improve their professional and technical skills.

The process by which Magnum established its values statement was less participative than Acme's IT team. The process was a great deal more top-down and is, for that reason, less effective than Acme's.

key concept

A clearly understood sense of *vision*, as we saw previously, provides the pull of a mutually understood destination for employees and colleagues.

A clearly understood and consistently supported set of *values* provides a framework, a set of mutually agreed controls, if you like; an agreement about the way we do things around here.

11 Assessing the implications of strategic intent

ASSESSING THE IMPLICATIONS OF STRATEGIC INTENT

Figure 11.1

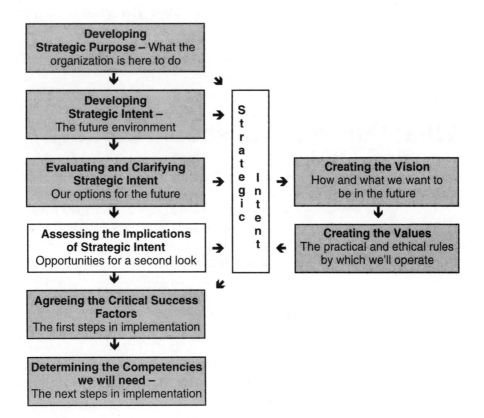

Before we move into implementation, we need to have a final look at strategic intent. Figure 11.1 shows where we are in the strategy development process.

Once we have established and agreed purpose – what we are here to do, and strategic intent – where we will concentrate our energies so that we can deliver our purpose long term, we need to stop a moment and reflect on what we have undertaken. This provides a kind of a breather – a short break between the major activities of determining strategic intent on the one hand, and planning for implementation on the other.

It really is to allow the dust to settle, to think a little more about the implications, to anticipate the planning process and, if we have scared ourselves half to death, to allow for some modification or second thoughts.

There are a couple of ways of testing the integrity of what we have identified as our strategic intent. Will it do for us what we need it to? Will it do all we need it to? Is it overkill? Is it too difficult? Is it too easy? This chapter helps answer those questions.

What this chapter should achieve

- You will learn to use an analytical tool called the Ansoff matrix.
- Using this matrix allows you to ask yourself a number of questions which help test the practicality of what you have in mind and particularly whether you have enough information.
- We will also look at a pro and con analysis which helps decision-making.
- You might end up with some modifications to your strategic intent, or you might decide to slightly change priorities.
- If, as recommended, you involve your people, you will be going well down the road to initiate change processes.

The process

- First we look at the Ansoff matrix to understand what it can do for us.
- Next we plot the elements of our strategic intent on to the matrix so that we know the implications of what we are intending.
- We use our friends at Acme to demonstrate the use of the matrix.
- We use Magnum to look at the simpler, and possibly more familiar, pro and con analysis matrix.

This part of the strategy development process should, ideally, fall a few days after the group has agreed the strategic intent. It is probably best conducted as a meeting rather than a facilitated workshop and it is best positioned by the leader manager as a review process after which some purposeful planning has got to take place.

The Ansoff matrix

This is an elderly but highly reliable tool and anybody, even with the vaguest idea of strategy, has heard of the Ansoff matrix (Figure 11.2) so you need to be able to use it to build

Figure 11.2
The Ansoff matrix

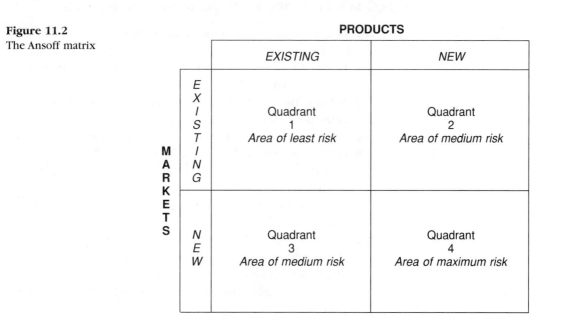

your credibility. More importantly it helps us get an idea of how difficult and effective our product and market strategies will be.

Interpreting the quadrants

Quadrant 1: existing products sold to existing markets

This is a low-risk strategy but questions to ask are:

- Is this business as usual?
- Will it provide the growth needed?
- Is the market growing fast enough, or will you have to increase your share?
- What makes you think you can increase share (your gain is one or more competitors' loss)?
- What will competitors do – how will they retaliate?
- What will increase share cost?
- What might a price war cost?
- How long can you continue to do this? What are the limits to growing the market? (Think how the product might change because of technology; think how the competitors might change because of globalization.)

Quadrant 2: new products to existing markets

This is a medium-risk strategy and questions to ask are:

- Is/are the new product(s) going to sell in the markets – what research have you done?
- What is the competitive advantage this new product will offer over those products sold in the market already?
- Have you got the price of the new products right?
- Can you buy/make, market and distribute the new product(s) at the price you have in mind and still make a profit?
- Can you buy or make enough of the product if it really takes off?
- Have you got the logistics of the new product right? (Procurement, warehousing, supply chain, channels, after-sales service etc.)
- Can your people handle (sell, support, service etc.) the product?

- What happens if existing suppliers of that product start a price war; can you afford it? For how long?
- How will you know whether it has worked or not worked?
- What happens if it doesn't work? What's your fallback position?

Quadrant 3: existing products to new markets

This is a medium-risk strategy and questions to ask are:

- How well do you know the market you intend to penetrate (size, buying habits, channels used etc.)?
- What do your people know about this new market; can they sell, support and service it?
- How much does it cost to reach this new market?
- How will those competitors who are serving the market now retaliate?
- Can you afford to fight it out with them? Price, margins, marketing spend?
- What is it about your product that will give it competitive advantage over the products of existing suppliers to the market? Are you sure?
- Who besides you is likely to enter this new market with similar product? (Think globally!)
- What rules are you setting yourself – limits to committing resource against expected return? How will you know if it is working?
- How will you know if it is not working?
- What is your fallback if it does not work?

Quadrant 4: new products to new markets

This is a maximum-risk strategy so you need to ask:

- Given the risk this strategy implies, is there not an easier way?
- What have you done/will you do to minimize risk – market analysis, competitor analysis, customer analysis, test marketing, product prototyping etc.?
- What parameters are you putting around spend and return; is there a progressive marketing/development plan so that you can assess results before spending more?
- What are you going to do to get your people up to speed on the market(s) and the product(s)?
- What is the fallback?

ASSESSING THE IMPLICATIONS OF STRATEGIC INTENT

Using Ansoff's matrix

The questions above are by no means comprehensive. What the matrix does for the user is to highlight a proposed set of strategic intentions and to cause you to think about them in terms of products and markets. This is a traditional approach to strategic planning and on its own is misleadingly simplistic. None the less it is a set of facets of the strategy which need to be examined.

Acme's IT team confronted the exercise as a group. This is what happened.

Acme's IT team and the Ansoff matrix

The group looked at their six separate strategic intentions (see Example in Chapter 9) and balked at the exercise because:

- they were not 'selling'
- they were not selling 'products'
- they had no choice about 'markets'.

Pressed to think in terms of their strategic intention in these terms they came up with the following:

Product or service	Market	Quadrant	Comment
Current product – installation, maintenance, software support and troubleshooting of office-based IT systems.	Existing users	1	This was low-risk current activity – we are good at it, but this phase of activity was just about completed. Minor software updates etc. will be added over time.
IT and systems consultancy. *Somewhere between a new and an existing product – more, we hope, towards the new than the existing.*	Existing users	1 to 2	Within the office, dealing with finance, and Sales and Marketing we will need to find ways of developing and demonstrating consultancy skills as distinct from the Mr Fixit services we provide now.

Product or service	Market	Quadrant	Comment
An IT strategic plan to serve Acme through to 2002. *We are not too sure what this plan might look like. It is definitely new product ground for us though the Acme top team are already users of our IT office systems.*	Acme top team	2	The top team would not recognize an IT strategic plan coming from us as an existing product. To win the right to range across the whole of Acme, a necessary condition to develop the plan, the top team will have to be sold and convinced. *No mean task.*
Computer integrated manufacturing. *It is clear that CIM will have to be of the products we will be selling if we are to provide competitive advantage for the organization.*	Manufacturing plant (who have not used us before).	4	This is certainly high risk – we simply do not have the IT skills in manufacturing which would allow us to 'consult'. There is no option but to serve this market, though, if we are to fulfil our purpose.
Computer integrated data/decision support systems. *This is a product we will have to supply. Not sure what it looks like; in a bigger organization it would be a SAP or an Oracle system – the ability to access and retrieve data and information within any phase of the business by any potential user in the business. Sometimes this is called **linking the board room to the shop floor.***	Some existing users, some new.	3 to 4	Again the team is concerned at how little we know in the area. Again we will not be fulfilling their purpose unless we can get our heads around it.

Acme's IT team discovered from this exercise that the strategic intent they had devised for themselves was causing them to play in each of the Ansoff matrix boxes. Traditionally this is the route to oblivion because not only is one embracing every conceivable level of risk, but also the complexity of what is being undertaken loses the clarity of focus which a business needs and which will orientate and direct the effort of employees.

This was a dismaying exercise for Acme's IT department. Whereas the activities of devising the main thrusts of strategic intent had been challenging, fun and a bit heroic, the realities with which the Ansoff matrix caused them to grapple inserted a degree of pragmatism which sobered them and showed them just how far they would have to go if they were to fulfil their strategic intent and the strategic vision.

Magnum Motors and the Ansoff matrix

Magnum found the Ansoff matrix less useful in that their strategy was relatively simpler.

Maintaining their share of the up-market business was essentially a Quadrant 1 (existing products to existing markets) activity, and hence low risk. When they put the Quadrant 1 questions to themselves it brought no important additional insights. They are well aware that their activity in their present markets is essentially a holding operation, and potentially an expensive one as the market shrinks.

Interesting discussions arose on the other main market/product plank of the strategic intent, entering the £9,999.99 market, i.e. a Quadrant 4 maximum-risk strategy. Could the risk be minimized by acquisition rather than by setting up a new dealership? The decision turned out to be a lot more complex and Magnum found it helpful to use the pro con matrix.

The pro and con matrix

This matrix aids decision-making when there are a number of possible variables affecting a decision. It is a useful means of building the collective views of a group into a coherent format so that a decision can be taken, or so that critical components of the decision can be identified.

It is best used by a manager/facilitator/team leader, interacting with a group and building the matrix in a visible real-time way, on a flip chart for example.

Basically the thinking behind it is to group positive and negative aspects of two potential courses of action in a way that makes them transparent. Here is Magnum's use of the tool.

Magnum Motors and the pro and con matrix

Figure 11.3

Buy existing dealership	Set up new dealership
+ Advantages +	**+ Advantages +**
• Proven market, known revenues • Faster – no need to look for sites • Buy existing expertise sales & service • Inherit an existing manufacturer relationship • Possibly easier to raise investment cash	• No bad habits to change – do it our way • Less expensive • Establish own brand of relationship with chosen manufacturer • Create own reputation with customers rather than inherit one
– Disadvantages –	**– Disadvantages –**
• Expense, especially of overpriced and probably misnamed 'good'will • Need to reduce the cost base – firing staff to access the synergy of the two businesses – little appetite for resulting blood bath or cost of doing it • Rehabilitation of a bruised and battered workforce following above • Dealerships known to be for sale were not franchisees of chosen manufacturers	• Hard to find suitable sites especially ones close to where we are (where best economies would result) • Time and management resource taken to develop site • Harder to attract investment in brand new dealership • Learning the ropes with a new Manufacturer • Hiring, training, and developing a new workforce • Risk, risk and then again risk

Magnum, as you can see, had by this time been sold on the idea of four-part analytical boxes.

Using the Ansoff matrix
The Ansoff matrix compels a consideration of the strategy within the context of products or services being offered, and the markets to which they are being offered. These considerations obviously lie at the heart of any strategic intent though they do not of themselves constitute a strategy.

Using the matrix exposes further facets of the strategic intent, and tends to shed more light on what needs to happen.

Using the pro and con matrix
The pro and con matrix helps clarify, make transparent and partially evaluate (+ or −) a number of variables which may affect a decision.

In both of the case studies we have used, this phase of the strategy-building process – assessing the implications of the strategic intent – was crucially important as a front end to the next stage – agreeing the critical success factors. The analyses each team performed in large measure determined where the priorities would lie in building CSFs.

12 Agreeing the critical success factors

Figure 12.1

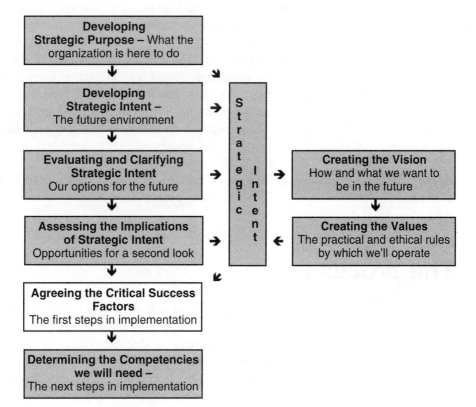

A critical success factor, in the sense we are using it here, is a broad objective which must be achieved in order to move you forwards towards your strategic intent. We call it a 'broad' objective because a CSF is actually an umbrella under which a number of individual objectives need to be achieved. This is particularly the case when achieving the CSF rests in the hands of several people or even several teams or units.

It will come as no surprise that CSFs which are determined jointly by those responsible for achieving them work much better than when these are simply handed down from on high. Again the processes of debate, of involvement, of participation all help clarify and place the strategic intent into an operating context. Critical success factors help establish the things that I have to focus on, the way I will allocate my time and, above all, why it is important that I do so.

What this chapter should achieve

- By the end of this section you will understand what a critical success factor is and how it is different from an objective.
- You should have learned to break down the key items of your strategic intent into critical success factors.
- You will also have positioned yourself for the start of action planning to implement your strategic intent.
- You should, if you carried out the Activities with your people, have galvanized them into an enthusiastic implementation mode.
- Everybody involved in the process will feel a bit better to be on familiar planning ground.

The process

- The chapter revolves around an Activity which is assumed to take place in a workshop format, led by the manager or team leader.
- Activity 12.1 moves into action planning.
- Case study materials from both Acme (for the operating unit within an organization) and Magnum (for the

example of the whole business) provide, as they have previously, examples rather than right answers. The intention is to illuminate the potential diversity of result, rather than specify outcomes.

● Two interviews at the end of the chapter, one from each of the case study subjects, shed some additional light on the whole strategy development process.

More about critical success factors

Graphically what is going on is shown in Figure 12.2.

It is important to realize that the strategy development process we have been undertaking has been progressively turning up new perspectives and shedding additional light on a solid core of organization or unit imperatives. It is unusual in most strategy development exercises for this solid core of imperatives - the things we know must be done - to change much during the process.

Rather, what we have gone through tends to reconfirm our gut feelings, to illuminate better what we know to be necessary, to

Figure 12.2

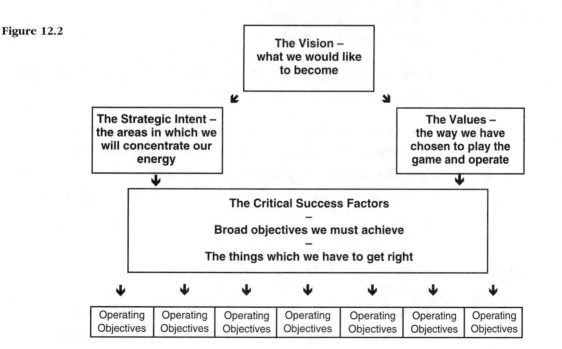

provide further context for what must be done. Often it also opens up a new understanding of consequences. One of the reasons that we continually advocate that these activities are undertaken by a team is that, during this time, a shared understanding of what must be done not only in broad outline but in detail and nuance is building. Without this shared understanding and without this depth of understanding the change processes which are being set up will not function. To achieve change, the leader must win the comprehension of his or her people, not merely their compliance. The strategic development process develops this comprehension.

Try this facilitated Activity.

12.1 Establishing the critical success factors

Step 1   *Assemble the main output documents you have achieved so far:*

- *the purpose statements*
- *the vision statements*
- *the values statements*
- *the strategic intent statements.*

It pays also to have handy some of the other working papers you have developed. Often needed are:

- *the outputs from Activity 9.2 (drawing conclusions from information) where you listed 'underlying statements, implications and emerging strategic intent'*
- *the outputs from the Ansoff matrix problem-solving session.*

Finally assemble your team for a three- or four-hour session.

Step 2   *Explain what you are here for:*

To determine the critical success factors – the broad objectives we must achieve to meet our strategic intent.

Tell them what you know about critical success factors. Tell them that from the outputs of this session you expect to be able to agree quarterly or half-yearly objectives with each person or operating unit, in other words a short-term operating plan.

Step 3   *Reread the* **purpose statement** *– invite comment.*
Reread the **vision statement** *– invite comment.*
Reread the **values statement** *– invite comment.*
Reread the **strategic intent statements** *– invite comment.*

You should not get a lot of comment on these if the steps outlined in the Activities which have generated them have been followed.

Step 4   *Divide the group into subgroups if possible. Allocate to each subgroup one or more of the strategic intent items. Sometimes there are clusters of closely related individual strategic intentions so put these together under the charge of a group.*

Brief the groups as follows:

Take a future perspective, say in five years' time. Imagine that we have been spectacularly successful in having achieved that strategic intention. Looking back, describe the main things we did to achieve that success.

Think practical things – think nuts and bolts – think operationally. Do not think how tos – think whats.

Allow them an hour and then take feedback.
Record feedback on a headline and definer basis (writing in the past tense helps, remember you are looking back from success) – see the case studies which follow.
Combine similar items of feedback – often the 'headline' is the same but a few more definers must be added.
These are your critical success factors. Review them, discuss them, ask if they are enough, too much, feasible, challenging enough, interesting enough, will they really contribute to achieving the strategic intent etc.

Step 5   *Divide the critical success factors between subgroups and ask them to turn these into a series of action plans defined as:*

- *breaking the critical success factor into a series of measurable sequential objectives*
- *defining the measure in 'measurable'*
- *addressing the resources which will be needed.*

Allow an hour, take feedback, invite volunteers.
Reach agreement about how you will incorporate the results of this meeting into the organization's or unit's objective-setting procedures.

Let us take a look at how Acme's IT team managed this Activity.

Acme IT team's critical success factors

Skills upgrade
- Created multiple centres of specialist, functional expertise among team e.g. manufacturing, SAP etc.
- Fast-track learning for each centre of expertise.
- Created 'space'/mobilized resources for fast-track development.
- Enlisted suppliers' help.
- Created learning objectives for each team member which were monitored and achieved.

Gained Acme top team credibility as strategic resource
- Carefully prepared presentation to top team.
- Undertook company-wide successful IT strategic review which was accepted by top team.

Demonstrated our purpose
- Provided measurable productivity improvement in 'Acme client' areas.
- Provided measurable customer satisfaction improvement in *internal* Acme client areas.

- Provided measurable customer satisfaction improvement for Acme *external* clients.
- Achieved measurable and extremely high ROI on IT investment.

Outsourced routine work at competitive rate and acceptable levels of service

- Spun off segment of the team and/or found first-rate external contractors.
- Had the systems to evaluate, control and achieve added value from outside contractors.
- Created/enabled confidence of internal Acme users in outside contractors.

Reduced operating cost

- Established some 'Moore's law' of cost reduction – pecentage of Acme overhead? Percentage Acme revenue? Actual number? Headcount? Etc.
- Made the Moore's law happen.

Maintained/enhanced team morale

- Rewarded team.
- Provided valid and valued individual development.
- Developed synergy – team strengths.
- Parties and celebrations.

Achieved highly productive relationship with suppliers

- Identified areas in which we would need partnership-type relationships (as distinct from buyer supplier-type relationships).
- Defined what we meant by 'partnership' in each area.
- Found suppliers capable of, and willing to, sustain partnership.
- Lived together happily ever after.

In general the Acme IT team were pleased with their critical success factors, though dismayed at the amount they had to achieve and also at the degree of change which would be necessary.

Having identified these critical success factors the team was keen to move on to establishing action plans and objectives.

It is often the case in strategy-building processes that people become frustrated by those activities which appear to have qualitative outputs. Most of us spend our business lives in more quantitative, pragmatic, facts-based activities. As the strategy development moves from helicopter mode towards concrete next steps; as it moves from future-focused thinking to what-to-do-by-Wednesday, people become more engaged and more enthusiastic simply because they are on more familiar ground.

Below is an edited summary of the Acme's response to Step 5 of Activity 12.1, determining the action plan.

Acme IT team's action plans

After some debate the team decided that they could not, as a group handle the critical success factor about reduced operating cost. Responsibility for this was handed to the team leader. It was further felt that with a probable major reorganization of individual responsibilities, different supplier thinking, possible spin-off and outsourcing of some team members etc., cost reduction should be reconsidered when some of the dust settled.

The team also decided to group the following CSFs together:

Gained Acme top team credibility as strategic resource.

Demonstrated our purpose.
It was felt that the multiple 'measurabilities' which the latter CSF suggested was actually the key to gaining Acme's top team's confidence in the IT team.

Skills upgrade.

Maintained/enhanced team morale.
These were seen as having elements of similarity though they were not identical or different ways of saying the same thing. Given the huge amount the team had to do, though, they could run on the same tracks for the time being.

Outsourced routine work at competitive rates and acceptable levels of service.

Achieved highly productive relationship with suppliers.
The first CSF about outsourcing was seen as a subset of the second CSF. In planning terms, however, the definers in the second CSF represented the front end of an action plan.

In the action plan which is reproduced in part below, two columns which appeared in the original are omitted. They were 'By (date)' and 'Responsibility': the first is self-evident, the second specified the name of the person on the team who took responsibility for delivering the objective even though others might be involved.

The team found that inserting the strategic intent which the objective supported was a good point of orientation and helped to develop the disciplines of their strategic thinking.

Acme IT team's action plans continued

Figure 12.3

CSF	Objectives	Resources needed	Strategic intent
Gained Acme top team credibility as strategic resource Demonstrated our purpose	Conduct interview with each member of top team to determine their expectations of IT in the company's strategy Conduct interviews with each function head to determine their expectations of IT in the future Devise a presentation to top team incorporating or adjusting their expectations and positioning the IT team's competence to support the strategy and serve the needs of function heads. Plan to define 'measures' we would incorporate and how they related to strategy Make presentation and ASK FOR RIGHT TO PROCEED WITH DRAWING UP AN IT STRATEGIC PLAN	Access to top team to be positioned by (Director to whom IT team reported) Time to set up, conduct & assimilate interviews Access to (Director to whom IT team reported) to dry run, test assumptions, seek clarification but especially to help address the 'measures' problem	Position ourselves as credible IT systems and consultancy resource with all functional departments To develop a strategic plan for IT and Systems to 2002 ALSO SEE CHARTER VALUES: ● Commitment to customers ● Commitment to Acme

CSF	Objectives	Resources needed	Strategic intent
Skills upgrade Team morale	Devise department-wide learning plan with specified targets as below: Designate major areas in which we must develop our skills – e.g. manufacturing, SAP etc. Allocate one or more areas to specified people Set objectives with each person to investigate and build information/resource base in each area – ALSO Identify main suppliers in each area – see *Productive relationships with suppliers* below Set learning objectives for each person including formal courses/training education etc.	Departmental meeting to thrash out areas and allocate Personnel/training for data on available courses Personnel/training for budget for training/education/ resource acquisition Bonus cash for meeting learning objectives	Upskill intellectual base of the department SEE ALSO CHARTER VALUES • Commitment to our people
Outsourced routine work at competitive rates	Identify current team activities and classify as 'core' or 'capable of being outsourced' Define levels of service required for outsourceable services Identify potential suppliers and invite informal tenders Compile comparative costs and review	A team meeting Time to write specifications Team agreement to specifications	Assure continuity of IT installation, training, maintenance etc., i.e. scope of current activity POSSIBLY BUT NOT CERTAINLY To reduce our cost base
Achieved highly productive relationships with suppliers	Review each supplier's performance in consultation with main user Conduct review with each supplier – feed back our performance experience – outline our Charter commitments – outline our learning needs (see above) – request added value	Time by (specified person) to gather and document performance data Time for reviews and evaluation of results	Manage our relationships/ alliances with bureaus to learn and achieve added value SEE ALSO CHARTER VALUE • Commitment to suppliers

What the Acme IT team now has is a set of plans and objectives covering an unspecified period but, as it happens, within Acme's normal objective-setting framework – i.e. six monthly. Names of people within the team responsible, though not shown here, are specified in the original and so are dates for completion.

It is important to note that this plan is fairly loose – it initiates action on all the CSFs (except cost reduction) but it remains open as to next steps. As time goes on the CSFs in the left-hand column will change; but the strategy-building process probably means that the strategic intent, and the values where adduced, will remain constant for a far longer period of time.

Magnum Motors' critical success factors

Resolved buy existing or set up new dealership quandary

Raised investment money
- Created an acceptable ownership/investor relationship with an acceptable long-term partner.
- Raised a cheap medium-term credit line from bank.
- Raised additional investment from current owners.

Bought/set up a dealership, new and used cars for [current manufacturer's] lower-priced offering and [specified new manufacturer] – operated it profitably by getting the cost saving from advantages of operating the two dealerships
- Implemented decision *fast*.
- Moved rapidly to achieve cost savings.

Developed sophisticated, effective low-cost direct marketing system
- Got people into the showroom.
- Improved salespeoples' conversion rate.
- Created high-trust, long-term relationships.

Developed uniquely effective customer care programme
- Identified where customer satisfaction *really* lies – the key components.
- Adapted facilities, systems, service reliability and staff behaviour – and everything else necessary to deliver these CSF components consistently.

Formed discreet but influential user group
- Enlisted support from key [manufacturer] dealerships.
- Did not arouse the suspicion of [the manufacturer].
- Influenced what the user group did, i.e. our agenda.
- Did not disclose our own strategy.

Magnum went on to put together their action plan. Again the version which follows is edited and omits two important columns – the name of the person or people responsible for the objective, and the date by which it was to be completed.

Magnum also chose not to deal with the question of the resource each of the objectives might need.

Figure 12.4

Magnum Motors' action plans

CSF	Objectives	Strategic intent
Resolved the buy existing/set up new dealership quandary	Create financial model covering: • buy a dealership • set up a dealership . . . for each show: • capital cost • operating cost at X% margin and A and B revenue levels . . . separately identify: • cost saving arising from joint operation of two dealerships • in the case of buy option, the cost of reorganizing to make cost savings above Confirm to [new manufacturer] our intention to seek/acquire franchise • gauge reaction – get their input • ascertain whether they know of any dealerships for sale Retain [estate agent] to search for suitable sites – site definition to be closely specified Approach A, B and C (all major supermarkets) with idea of our operating a new/used car lot on their existing/new sites	Enter the £9,999.99 priced market

CSF	Objectives	Strategic intent
Raised investment cash	Do financial model comparing part sale (two percentages specified) and payment of dividend, to long-term debt repayment *This objective specified a number of possible investors who would be approached with the business plan* Approach bank with business plan and get reaction to credit line	Enter the £9,999.99 priced market
Bought/set up a dealership . . . stress on doing it fast	*The objective here was stated as some internal organizational changes. Magnum's Operations Director took over a number of the Managing Director's day-to-day tasks. The Service Director took over others. The idea was to free the MD to concentrate all his energies on the set up/acquisition*	Enter the £9,999.99 priced market
Developed sophisticated, effective low-cost marketing system.	Purchase and proceed with the implementation of (a specified software package designed for highly targeted direct mail activity) Put all floor salespeople through (a specified ethical selling course). Put (specified names responsible for Corporate sales) through Strategic Selling Course	Maintain our share of the up-market car business rather than expand it SEE ALSO Magnum's Code of Conduct – on customer expectations and undertakings about unethical practice
Developed uniquely effective customer care programme	Retain [name specified] consultants to conduct a focus group programme to determine key areas in which we could excel in customer care Take this as input to whatever organizational/systems/staff behaviour changes we need to achieve high customer satisfaction	Build new and improved levels of customer service . . . best in the business Maintain our share of the up-market car business rather than expand it SEE ALSO Magnum's Code of Conduct – on customer expectations and Magnum's relationships with the manufacturer – being the flagship dealer
Formed discreet but influential user group	*The objectives here are too specific as to which other dealers should be involved and the nature of the agenda to be of much use to the reader*	User group of other manufacturer dealerships to interact productively with the manufacturer

Interviews with case study clients: the Acme IT team

Q: Now that you have finally got an action plan, do you feel the lengthy strategy building process was worth it?

A: Absolutely – it is the best thing we've done as a team.

Q: What makes it the best thing you've done as a team?

A: First, we all enjoyed it though we did seem to be losing the plot on a few occasions. Second, while we were and are a hard-working, effective team, and we're proud of what we do, I don't think we've ever looked at our role the way the process forced us to look at it.

Q: What, if anything, did you gain from looking at your role strategically?

A: A number of things came clear. We realized we were vulnerable because of our cost. We realized that we should really take a very different view of the future – become strategists in fact. We realized that we simply lacked the skill sets we would need longer term. What really changed the game was having to think about the future – and realizing that we had to take charge of the future.

Q: Does the team behave differently now from the way it behaved before?

A: I think we've got some way to go to get there. Old habits die hard and we tend to lapse back into fire-fighting every now and then. What has changed, though, is the longer-term stuff we're working on. And while this stuff is not easy to work with, it is a lot easier than not knowing what we should be working on long term.

Q: What are the downsides of the strategy development process you have been through?

A: It took a lot of time. When you look at the action plans now (and they're brilliant, incidentally), you realize that we should have been able to get there in an afternoon. You feel we either did or should have known all this stuff all along. There's a kind of 'so what' about it. Did we do all this work to end up with, say, three, four useful pages?

Q: How are you dealing with that perception?

A: Well I don't mean it as a criticism of the process, I mean that we feel ... I suppose the word is 'embarrassed' that it took all that effort and refocusing our thinking to bring out something we should have known all along. Maybe we did know it, but we sure as hell could not have articulated it nor were we 'doing' it.

Q: Would you do it again?

A: We have to. It should be faster in the future because we're clear about some of the big picture elements like purpose and vision and values. But I guess we'll have to revisit these things as well. Will we?

Q: You bet your sweet life you will ... But it *will* be faster next time round.

Interviews with case study clients: Magnum Motors

Magnum's feedback on the process comes in a letter:

... you asked for our views on the strategy development process we have just been through – here goes:

To be frank we did not find it easy. It generated a lot of heat, and I was under pressure from at least one of my team to abandon it ... We also thought it took a lot of time, and in the beginning especially, we felt we were starting too far back.

In the event, though, it surfaced the two critical things we have to do; maintain our share in the market we know and enter the £9,999.99 market.

Now if you asked my colleagues what they felt about this they'd say they all knew that anyway. It may or may not be true. The fact is that having been through the process we're actually doing something about it. More, and this is a real payoff, we are agreed what we should do.

If you look at it that way we have taken a giant step forward.

You also asked me to comment on whether it has changed the way we work. The answer is that we are doing different things to support the two main strategic intentions. What I am not sure about is whether we have learned to think about what we do in the terms you advise:

. . . is this consistent with Purpose?
. . . is this going to move us closer to our Vision?

On the other hand I think the Values exercise was really important for us. What is more I think it impressed the staff when we came back and talked about it.

Finally you asked whether we would do it again . . . well we have to, don't we!

13 Determining the competencies we will need

Figure 13.1

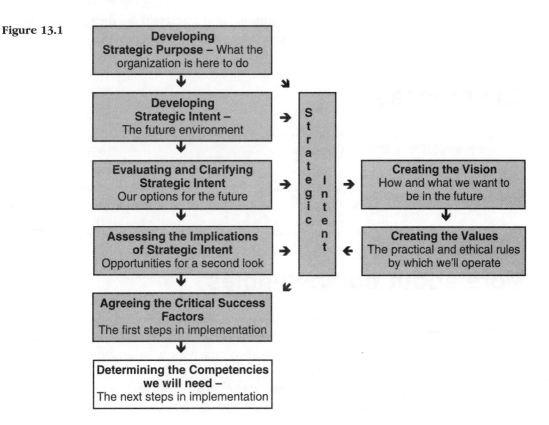

This is the last stage in the strategy development process which we have been following. With purpose clear, with the best possible view of the future environment, with an agreed strategic intent, critical success factors agreed and an action plan developed, we must now assess the skills and competencies we will need for successful implementation.

What this chapter should achieve

- We will agree what competencies are and the different ways in which they can be looked at within an organization.
- You will learn to distinguish between the knowledge necessary to develop competence and the skills to display competent behaviour.
- You will develop a competency framework for your unit or organization which you may need to add into your action planning.
- Your people will have a clear idea of the contribution each will have to make towards achieving the strategic intent because, by implication, each will see the relevance of his or her own development to the action plan.

The process

- Following the presentation of a simple competency model we move to a collaborative Activity.
- The Activity is designed to develop a competency framework for the unit or organization.
- We use the Acme IT team to see an application, and we see how and why Magnum differed in their approach.

More about competencies

When we discussed successful modern strategies in Chapter 5 we defined competencies as: 'The strengths or capabilities we will have to develop to manage our strategic intent.'

To help us deal with ideas involved, we grouped competencies under three headings:

1 *Generic competencies* – competencies without which no serious organization can imagine continuing; things like continuous quality improvement, continuous process improvement, continuous customer satisfaction improvement, the ability to change fast, the ability to learn fast, etc.

When we discuss competencies at this level, we are referring to organizational competencies, those things which the organization is capable of achieving through the systems it has put in place and the skills which the employees bring to bear as they operate the systems.

Sometimes these are called *core competencies* because they lie at the heart of the organization's operations.

2 *Industry-specific competencies* – those which are necessary for the organization to participate in the industry. Most industries establish professional or vocational standards; things which people should be able to do to be employed in the industry. In addition many industries are looking for commitment to continuing professional development (CPD), so that employees in the industry are continuously upskilling themselves.

3 *Components of competitive advantage* – those competencies which consistently enable the organization to outperform its competitors. They might be generic, core organizational capabilities developed to levels of great excellence.

The consistent quality and reliability of Japanese motor cars is a core competence shared by Toyota, Nissan, Honda and Mitsubishi, and one they are able to achieve no matter where they manufacture. The excellence of service of Singapore Airlines is a competence which provides competitive advantage.

Importantly the potential buyer must believe that this competence is a consistently reliable characteristic of the supplier's capability – only then does the competence confer a measure of competitive advantage.

All these categories of competency come together when we consider them in the light of the strengths and capabilities we will need to achieve our strategic intent.

It has been a key consideration as we have developed the strategy that people responsible for implementation are involved in the process and help frame, define and inform the results. This involvement, because it provides context, understanding and ownership, is the fuel of the engine of change. The other requirement of the engine is a lubricant, something that enables the parts to move together and minimizes friction. Competence, the *ability* to do what I understand needs to be done, is that lubricant.

While there a number of ways of viewing competence – we alluded in Chapter 5 to the difficulty most organizations have in establishing their core competencies – strategic intent provides us with a key to defining the competencies needed and also helps indicate priority. The pragmatic, actionable access provided through the window of strategic intent is, in my view, one of the most effective means of building a competence framework and the development programme which the organization will need.

A competency model

In Britain the idea of competence has been developed to provide the basis of formal qualification, the National Vocational Qualification (NVQ) movement. Huge sums of money and great effort has been committed to identifying Vocational Qualifications in various occupational areas and at various levels of performance. Without going too deeply into the subject, we can borrow some key concepts in thinking about developing the competency model which will be needed for the implementation of our strategic intent. We can also delve into the considerable body of competence information which the NVQ system has already developed.

The model we will use is shown in Figure 13.2. *Note*: This is not the model which the NVQ system uses, it is recommended here for simplicity sake. Human Resource (HR) professionals would also regard this as grossly oversimplified. My experience is that it has helped line managers clarify their

Figure 13.2
A competency model

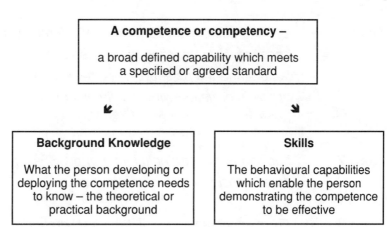

ideas so that they can interact from a more informed viewpoint with the HR people.

With this broad-brush model in mind try this outline Activity which will help establish the competencies you are going to need.

13.1 Developing a competency framework

You can conduct this Activity as a group or, to use time more efficiently, by having team members do it in advance and then agreeing a way forward at a meeting.

If you have a Human Resource function within the organization, they can generally do it for you. Remember, as a line manager it is important that you own the competence framework, understand how it contributes to strategic intent, and are ready to implement it through objective-setting, development planning and so on.

If you are a Human Resource person, you probably already have a number of sophisticated means of achieving the outcome of the Activity.

Step 1   *Use the action plan as a point of reference. This is valuable because it summarizes the strategic intent, the critical success factors and the objectives you have decided to set yourselves. All of this information will help illuminate the competencies you will need.*

Step 2   *Looking at the strategic intent and CSFs, list the broadly defined competencies which come to mind.*

Step 3   *For each competency, list the background knowledge you believe is necessary to demonstrate the competency.*

Step 4   *For each competency, list the skills you believe are necessary to demonstrate the competency.*

Step 5   *Next to each competency list the person, people or category of people who will need to be able to demonstrate it.*

Step 6   *Now is the moment to compare your views with others in the team and to synthesize your results.*

Step 7   *Write this up and you have the competency framework. You also have the front end of the development plan in that you have identified people who must develop the competency.*

Here is how the Acme IT team did.

Figure 13.3

Acme's competency framework

Competency	Knowledge base	Skills base
Consultancy skills	State of the art of major branches of IT (e.g. SAP, CIM, decision support systems etc.) Underlying thinking/logic behind each branch Major applications, successes and failures – benchmarks Key suppliers, practitioners	Questioning, listening, summarizing, 'discovering' or 'finding out' skills Presentation, feedback, skills ability to make logical recommendation Process skills – ability to lead a group
Project management	Available software – critical path analysis Best practice cases	People/change management skills Coaching teaching skills Risk reducing/ empowering skills
Purchasing/supplier relationship competencies – partnerships	Shape and nature of good supplier/purchaser relationships Contracting – legal aspects – mutual liabilities etc.	Negotiation skills Selling skills
Business process re-engineering	How you do it, i.e. processes and systems by which process re-engineering takes place Good case examples Best practice – benchmarks	Not known – what skills are needed?
Teamwork skills	Background to teaming Best/worst practice Kaizen Collective decision-making – consensus Team processes and team development	Skills of 'being a team member' Interpersonal skills Questioning skills, confronting skills
Strategic thinking, planning and behaving	Theoretical basis of strategy Strategy's heavy hitters: Levitt, Porter, Ohmae, Hamel and Pralahad etc. The analytical tools and models Contemporary thinking	Continue to hone and polish our already prodigious skills in the area of strategy development

Note the interesting addition of business process re-engineering to the competency framework. This arose because it was felt that as the proposed IT strategic plan was implemented it would affect internal processes at Acme. If the team was to fulfil its purpose, contribute to Acme's competitive advantage, IT-instigated process re-engineering was inevitable.

Magnum and the competency framework

Magnum declined to develop a competence framework. The top team felt that they were well aware of the training and development processes which would have to take place across the company.

On the hard side – vehicle servicing, the manufacturer and the potential new manufacturer both mandated training programmes, controlled quality and accredited successful performance.

On the softer side, some research had been done already, as was evident by the action plan, in which specific programmes were named for salespeople on the dealership floor and for those who were involved with corporate sales.

Magnum acknowledged that if they were to achieve their strategic intent of 'building new and improved levels of customer satisfaction ... the best in the business', they would probably be into some special form of competence development which would indeed cover both knowledge and skills bases. The objective they had set themselves, however, was to determine, through focus groups, the major components which would directly affect customer satisfaction. Until they had determined what they wanted, however, they chose to leave the competence framework in abeyance.

Moving to a development plan

The competency framework is, of course, the precursor to a development plan for each individual in the organization.

A development plan emerges after each employee and that employee's immediate supervisor have agreed his or her current level of ability against the competencies required and also a plan to bridge the gap has been devised.

Such a plan must, of course, have mutually agreed objectives which are measurable on as quantitative a basis as possible.

Implementing strategic intent will inevitably involve changes in the way people behave and the way they do their jobs. This will in turn involve a re-evaluation of their competence to do what is required of them to support the strategic intent.

The competence framework is a simple and effective tool to help define the development plans which will have to be put in place. Completing the exercise again sheds valuable light on the strategic intent itself providing more insight, more understanding and hence greater clarity for all concerned.

14 Measuring the effectiveness of your strategy

Traditional measures of organizational performance

The profit and loss account and the balance sheet remain the primary measures of most companies. They provide a common lens, honoured by long-standing and universal usage. They represents snapshots of organizational performance and if you look at the 'album', a few years' worth of profit and loss accounts and balance sheets, you get a picture of historical performance.

● The limitation of balance sheets and profit and loss accounts is, of course, that they measure and reflect only financial performance. It can be argued that financial performance is the only reasonable and defensible measure to take seriously since the continuity of the organization is directly contingent upon its financial performance. It can also be argued that the assets and liabilities of an organization are only understandable when they are translated into financial terms. This, too, would be a view hard to fault.

● What financial measures do not address is the potential success of the company in the future. That potential success is, of course, only as good as its strategy. We have already discussed the high mortality rate of even high-flying organizations, and it is fair to say that long-term survival rests upon having got *the* right, or *a* right, strategy in position and then being able to implement it.

- Measuring the strategy really has a twofold intention:

  - Is it happening? Are we doing what we decided to do? Are we achieving our critical success factors?
  - Is the strategy working? Have we got it right? As we actually deploy the strategic intent, is that producing the result we are looking for?

In the hypercompetitive environment in which we work, the second set of questions above must not only be asked more often, but they must also be answered sometimes on the slimmest of evidence. Good managers know when to be brave, when to tough it out through indicators which are negative or confusing. Good managers also know when to back away from and dismantle a strategy in favour of a new one.

Sometimes, too, the pressures of the investment community are hard to withstand. A profits warning will trigger a fall in share price, a fall in share price can alarm employees, alarmed employees tend to alienate customers, alienated customers take their custom elsewhere.

All the evidence is, as we said when we discussed the concept of organizational accountability, that organizations that manage all their stakeholder relationships effectively are those which survive and prosper. If stakeholders are not surprised, if they are aware of the major thrust of the organization's strategy, if they have been warned about potential consequences of that strategy, they will usually support the organization even if its primary indicators look temporarily unpromising.

Coca-Cola is a company much loved by its investors for the consistently excellent results it achieves. In 1997 Coke announced a change in its international strategy.

- It would be seeking to reduce the number of bottling plants it operated world-wide and consolidate its production in fewer, larger units which would ultimately be more effective.
- This move was coupled with the announcement that Coke would have to take a very substantial profits-denting charge against its current year profit and loss in order to implement this strategy.
- The announcement actually led to a rise in Coke's share price because investors felt that, longer term, Coke was pursuing the right strategy.

Some new approaches to measuring

First, let us get very clear about what it is we are measuring: we are measuring the effectiveness of our strategy and we are doing so against some general or universal sets of criteria which are common to all organizations. These criteria have been refined for us by Robert Kaplan and David Norton who in their books and journal articles have provided an exceptionally valuable set of general/universal criteria. Under the umbrella of each of these criteria, measures specific to our own particular strategy can be grouped. In the approach we have taken these measures would be our critical success factors and even the objectives in our action plans.

Kaplan and Norton's work is built around a concept called the *balanced score card* and in broad summary the four key areas or 'perspectives', to use their own word, for measuring the success of strategy are:

1 *Financial measures* – still the most important, because they are universal, widely understood and almost culture free. Traditionally financial measures are profitability and return on investment. However, organizations are being judged increasingly on the economic value they add. Shareholder return is usually critical for companies where ownership is widely held.

2 *Customer measures* – these embrace a number of possible applications though each is in some way related to customer satisfaction which lies at the heart of retaining customers and gaining market share through the acquisition of new customers.

3 *Internal measures* – cover the processes which the organization uses internally, i.e. all those things which are done to manufacture the product, provide the service, deliver to it to the market, etc. Internal measures relate to the productivity and efficiency with which the company operates. They relate to progressive improvement in quality and continuous reduction of cost.

4 *Learning and growth measures* – cover those areas where employee development, either through information or learning, can influence and enhance organizational performance.

To see the model at work, let us look at its application to the work done by our two case study organizations, Acme's IT team and Magnum Motors.

Acme IT team's alignment with generic measures

Figure 14.1

Financial measures

Reduce operating cost

Customer measures

Customer (including top team) see the IT team as a strategic resource

ALSO Charter values as they affected customers

Internal measures

Reduce operating cost
Outsourcing routine work
Productive supplier relationships

In fact the team saw their critical contribution to Acme as their ability to enhance the whole company's internal systems through the use of IT – thus providing Acme with a competitive advantage. This, you will recall, was the team's purpose

Learning and growth measures

Upskilling intellectual base of the department: departmental learning plan

Consultancy competencies
Project management competencies
Purchasing/supplier relationship competencies
Team competencies
Process re-engineering competencies

It is usually, as can be seen in Figure 14.1, quite easy to classify CSFs or objectives within the scope of this measuring system.

What is less easy is to devise a measure for each. In the event, most organizations go for two different types of measures:

- those associated with specific projects – all of the objectives in the Acme team's action plan fall quite comfortably into this category
- ongoing measures against which incremental performance is required. Acme devised, for example, a feedback questionnaire called their perceived strategic contribution (PSC) measure. This they applied and continue to apply to functional heads within the company looking to improve their overall ratings annually.

Magnum's alignment with generic measures

Financial measures

We already know that Magnum's top team owned about half of the company and were employed by it. Their interest was to increase the shareholder value of the business.

While the figures have not been disclosed in case reporting, there was a clearly articulated set of financial measures which the strategic intent was devised to deliver.

As we know, the strategic intent was slanted at investment, growth and expansion with a readiness to accept lower profitability in the short/medium term.

Customer measures

Magnum's 'manufacturer' has, as do all motor car franchisers, very highly developed Customer Satisfaction Indices. The manufacturer places, as they always do, great importance on this index and collects data directly.

Magnum had been a consistently good performer against this index but, as the strategy showed, they felt there were, as yet unrevealed, criteria by which they could achieve enhanced customer satisfaction over other of the manufacturer's dealerships. This is what they hoped to uncover in their focus groups.

Internal measures

Two categories exist here, the first well established. These are the systems and measures which assess productivity of the service function. The base measure is service revenue per capita.

The other sets of measures were less well defined. They rested in the sales areas and surfaced their objectives for targeted direct mail and salespeople's conversion rates.

Learning and growth measures

Magnum saw this area as the training programmes they had in mind for salespeople.

The Fix Right First Time commitment which supports customer satisfaction also rests on the skills of the service personnel. A consistently more sophisticated product requires consistently more sophisticated technical capability to which Magnum was committed and which it measures through the manufacturer's accredited training.

Figure 14.2

MEASURING THE EFFECTIVENESS OF YOUR STRATEGY

The case for measuring systems to drive strategy development

The four-part balanced scorecard has great value for:

- the simple comprehensiveness of the perspectives from which strategic success should be viewed (Finance, Customers, Processes and Learning). In a wide experience of strategy building, the concepts supporting this model turn out to be fairly robust.
- the integrity of the thinking it produces – 'What can I do and how can I measure the effectiveness of what I have done to improve and monitor my organization's or unit's performance in these four key areas?'

The balanced scorecard leads to another approach to strategy building and to establishing strategic intent. The steps in the process are shown in Figure 14.3.

Figure 14.3
A strategy-building process

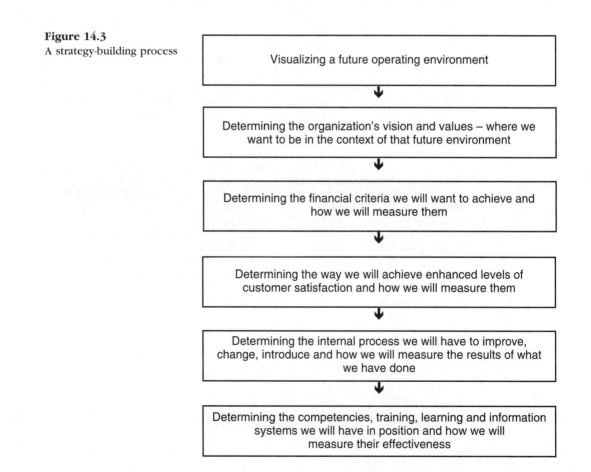

In effect, taking this approach to strategy building provides an alternative route to that which we have travelled so far. Teeing up a strategy development exercise from the four perspectives or areas of generic measurement is often a good top-up technique which is best undertaken a few months after the original exercise.

The reasons that the balanced scorecard approach to strategy building is risky as a starting point are:

- It focuses insufficiently on the all important *future perspective* which is essential if a viable strategic intent is to be devised.
- It makes the assumption that vision and values are in position already, whereas this is often not the case. Further it is rarely true that all the stakeholders share a congruent vision. It is for this reason that the first two steps are advocated in the strategy development model in Figure 14.3.
- It does not deal comprehensively with competition; it provides little opportunity (except implicitly) to envisage future markets with existing and new competitors exercising different kinds of influences in them.

On the other hand, once a group has gone through the pain of all that futuring, the balanced scorecard approach specifies some admirably pragmatic ways of approaching strategic implementation. It has value because serious measurement requires a level of co-ordination, alignment and agreement. The organization has to iron out the details, pay attention to the 'small print' and explore and resolve nuances of differences between people and between functional departments. This is beyond mere good housekeeping, it is about establishing consensus. Indeed, the way in which the model (see Figure 14.4) uses words like 'clarifying', 'communicating', 'linking', 'aligning', is the key to its power.

Perhaps one of the best ways of understanding how the use of the balanced scorecard concept facilitates the development of strategy is to use Kaplan and Norton's own excellent graphic which they entitle 'The balanced scorecard as a strategic framework for action'.

The model also addresses a fundamental human motivation; that is, that people will achieve results in areas where they

Figure 14.4
The balanced scorecard
(from Kaplan and Norton,
1996)

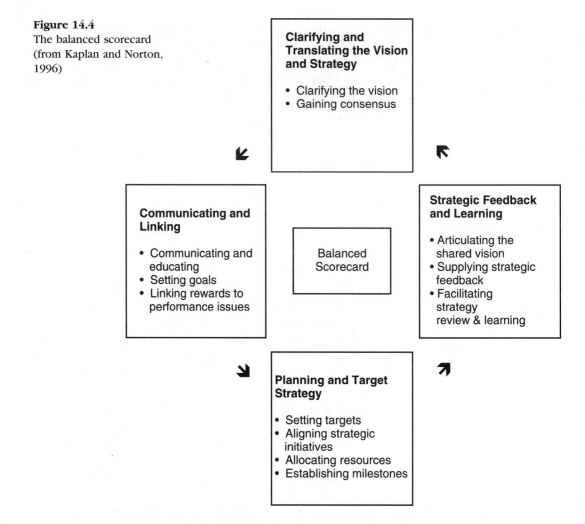

Clarifying and Translating the Vision and Strategy

- Clarifying the vision
- Gaining consensus

Communicating and Linking

- Communicating and educating
- Setting goals
- Linking rewards to performance issues

Balanced Scorecard

Strategic Feedback and Learning

- Articulating the shared vision
- Supplying strategic feedback
- Facilitating strategy review & learning

Planning and Target Strategy

- Setting targets
- Aligning strategic initiatives
- Allocating resources
- Establishing milestones

know they are being measured. Understanding and agreeing standards of attainment will cause people to behave differently so that they achieve the standard. In the choice of the priorities people establish for themselves, in the way they exercise discretion in actually doing their work, they will shape their activity to meet the standard.

It is in this ability to direct the work of employees without supervision or intervention that the practice of measurement is also at its most vulnerable, for if measures are not properly balanced the organization is at risk of skewing its performance. Consider the following table.

Measure		Potential consequence
Customer retention	➜	Insufficient resource (energy, time and money) devoted to new customer acquisition
New customer acquisition	➜	Insufficient resource (energy, time and money) devoted to customer retention
Quality improvement of existing products	➜	Resource deflected from new product development
New product development	➜	Quality improvement of existing products potentially neglected
Cost reduction	➜	Service improvement suffers

and so on.

It is for this reason that:

- the *balanced* nature of the scorecard is critical
- time and energy must be spent on *alignment* of measures
- the segment of the virtuous circle called *feedback and learning* is of critical importance.

Help

Measuring strategy means
– are we achieving our CSFs?
– is the strategy producing the results?

Four generic measures
– Financial – ROI, shareholder value, economic value added
– Customers – customer satisfaction, retention, acquisition
– Internal processes how you run the business inside – quality, productivity
– Learning and growth – employee development, information.
Together these make the *balanced scorecard*.

Two types of measure
– Outcomes of specific projects.
– Ongoing to judge incremental performance over time.

Potential for balanced scorecard approach to be used as basis for strategy development

Upsides
– Framework is simple, comprehensive, robust and highly pragmatic.

Downsides
– Lacks future focus.
– Assumes vision and values are agreed.
– Lacks competitor analysis.

Best used as top-up for strategy development.

Measurement can skew performance.

15 Aspiring to excellence

No exercise in strategy development should ignore the aspiration towards excellence, to achieve world class status, potentially to be the best. This chapter does not purport to provide the recipe, but it does assemble some views and models which the strategist should think about. If the strategic aspiration is more limited, why should it be?

Jack Welch of General Electric

Jack Welch is Chairman of General Electric (GE), by any criteria one of the world's most successful companies. In the *Fortune 500* for 1998 GE is the company with the highest market value, and with the fifth largest revenue It is a company which has, over the last decade, provided an average 24 per cent return to its investors.

General Electric has a vast range of separate businesses, from making jet engines to one of the most successful finance companies. It operates on many sites in many countries and it serves literally hundreds of different markets.

When he assumed the top job at GE Welch engaged on a programme of rationalization of its huge and varied portfolio of businesses. Over the years that Welch has been in charge, many businesses have been sold and many more were purchased.

Welch's guiding strategic principle in divestiture and acquisition has been that GE should not own a business which was not the best in its field, or capable of becoming the best.

The simplicity of this strategic principle, and the power with which it has driven GE, must lie at the heart of the company's spectacular success.

What achieves excellence?

Ever since Tom Peters and Robert Waterman wrote *In Search of Excellence* in the early 1980s, a sometimes lucrative subindustry has grown up with gurus purporting to identify the characteristics which are common to excellent or high-performing companies.

It is interesting to compare Peters and Waterman's list, which is one of the earliest (1982), with Goldsmith and Clutter-buck's list in their book *The Winning Streak* (1997):

Peters and Waterman: Eight principles	Goldsmith and Clutterbuck: Ten key balances for success
A bias for action – getting on with doing things rather than engaging in endless analysis	**Control vs autonomy** – giving people maximum freedom of action while not losing the advantage of the organization's size and momentum
Staying close to the customer – really knowing about the customer and being able to cater for his or her needs	**Long-term strategy vs short-term urgency** – tackling tomorrow's problems today; thinking strategically reduces long-term fire-fighting
Autonomy and entrepreneurship – creating small operating units and encouraging them to act independently	**Evolutionary vs revolutionary change** – focus on what is not working well and fix it before looking for new areas of break-through
Productivity through people – all employees aware of the importance of their effort and their contribution to success	**Pride vs humility** – being proud of your success but constantly careful not to become complacent
Hands-on, value driven – the top people very much involved with the heart of the business and holding strong beliefs about it	**Focus vs breadth of vision** – stick to the knitting by all means but be aware when change is necessary
Stick to the knitting – continuing to do the things the unit does best	**Values vs rules** – values are understood and govern decision-making at all levels, but there are still rules which tell employees what to do
Simple form, lean staff – flat organizations with simple structure	**Customer care vs customer count** – getting bigger means having more customers, balance this with your ability to look after them
Loose tight properties – creating real dedication to the central values and purpose of the organization but encouraging diversity and range of approach	**Challenging people vs nurturing them** – setting demanding targets for people while supporting and understanding them as well
	Leaders vs managers – both are important, but in high-performing companies more time is spent leading than managing
	Gentle vs abrupt succession – smooth changes at the top; continuity of the core values and strategy.

ASPIRING TO EXCELLENCE

Even in the use of the word 'balances' there is congruence between the Peters and Waterman approach and that of Goldsmith and Clutterbuck. Both advocate the need for the organization, for its leaders and for its employees to operate at some realistic point along a spectrum of possibilities (e.g. control through to autonomy). Goldsmith and Clutterbuck enshrine it in their thinking by expressing the components of excellence in terms of balances; Peters and Waterman refer to it as managing ambiguity and paradox.

What is interesting is that over a fifteen-year period the models identified are not substantially different although the environment in which organizations operate has, in fact, changed a great deal because of the accelerating impact of globalization, technology, customer choice and employee values.

key concept

Strategic thinking is very much about designing the climate and culture which will best suit the organization and enable it to achieve its strategic intent.

The sort of organization described in the models can usually be captured by the vision and values activities. Your people will usually contribute with enthusiasm and energy to building a picture of a flatter, more empowered organization.

Working towards this sort of model will not, of itself, create excellence, but coupled with a winning strategy it should get you close.

A more structured view of excellence

The need to create world-class companies has led to the development of more precise and prescriptive models of excellence than those of the gurus. The British Quality Foundation, drawing heavily on the US Malcolm Baldridge Award structure, has produced a model against which organizations can assess themselves and which provides a continuous benchmarking facility to enable them to measure improvement in their performance. The model is shown in Figure 15.1.

Figure 15.1
Model of
excellence

Leadership 100	People management 90	Processes 140	People satisfaction 90	Business results 150
	Policy and strategy 80		Customer satisfaction 200	
	Resources 90		Impact on society 60	

◄ Enablers ► ◄ Results ►

Enablers

Leadership – the way the behaviour of the top team and other leaders inspires, supports and promotes a climate of excellence

Policy and strategy – how the organization formulates, deploys and reviews strategy and turns it into action plans

People management – how the organization realizes the full potential of the employees in serving customers

Resources – how the organization's resources are deployed in the support of the strategy

Processes – how all the value adding activities in the organization operate and how they are reviewed and revised to assure continuous improvement

Results

Customer satisfaction – evidence of the way customers see the organization's products, services and customer relationships

People satisfaction – evidence of the employees' perception of the organization

Impact on society – what the organization is achieving in relation to the community. Perceptions of the organization's approach to quality of life, the environment, preservation of global resources

Business results – what the organization is achieving in relation to its planned objectives and the needs of its stakeholders

The scoring system, as can be seen, amounts to a potential 1,000, 500 each for Enablers and for Results. The relative weights of the component elements of the model are supposed to define the contributory importance of each.

There are two ways in which you can use this model:

1 You can enlist the services of the British Quality Foundation who will provide assessment material, benchmarking services and, ultimately, live assessors. If you win a UK Excellence award you get to shake the hand of the Princess Royal.

ASPIRING TO EXCELLENCE

2 You can use the model as a reference point against which you can think of the development activities for your own organization or operating unit. Its value lies in its comprehensiveness and the kind of checklist facility it provides to assure yourself that you have covered all the bases.

It is not necessarily true that organizations accept the relative weighting of the model's components, and some use it as a basis on which to build their own internal development systems, rather than as a metric against which to measure themselves.

Some organizations find the scope and comprehensiveness of this excellence model too overpowering. I recently heard the chief executive of an organization employing several thousand people describing with derision the 'pot plant improvement programme'. His point was that the culture or climate of continuous improvement can develop a life of its own and can lose sight of the priorities of the business.

In abandoning the model this chief executive moved more in the direction of the balanced scorecard approach but split the processes section into two divisions, one of which was safety, an area, because of the nature of the business, that was absolutely critical to its success.

It is also true that in most businesses continuous incremental improvement is not a sufficient strategy to assure viability. While every organization must devote resource and energy to improvement, whether product and service quality or internal processes, most also need to focus energy on breakthrough, on doing the new and different, on innovation.

Renewal, reinvention, strategic audacity are as important in a hypercompetitive environment. The need to balance the cash cow thinking of continuous improvement with the glittering potential of the wild blue yonder is an important component of survival.

Let us look at an interesting synthesis of many of these models, as embodied in the practice of a highly successful company.

Hewlett Packard Ltd

Hewlett Packard was founded in the UK in 1957. The company now employs over 5,000 people and contributes about £1.9 billion to the group's international revenues.

The company defines its strategy as 'the undefended hill', in other words, it seeks product areas where there are few or relatively weak competitors and then builds products of outstanding technical excellence.

Historically it has been able to rely on its ability to stay ahead technologically, but it acknowledges that this is increasingly difficult to do in the global marketplace.

Hewlett Packard was early into total quality management (TQM) but latterly is moving more towards an excellence model of its own called the quality maturity system (QMS).

At the heart of its model is a fourfold commitment to:

- continuous improvement
- innovation
- customer focus
- people satisfaction.

The balanced scorecard concept is also used at Hewlett Packard but in a version of its own.

The ability to select and synthesize various models and to adapt them to the specific culture and environment of Hewlett Packard is one of the means of the organization's outstanding success.

The effectiveness of the systems and culture it deploys to achieve excellence is simply described and mutually understood by all employees in the phrase 'the Hewlett Packard way'.

The drive to achieve excellence, to become world class, to be best in category is not only a legitimate aspiration for the strategist, whether for the organization or for the operating unit, it is absolutely to be encouraged.

Taking from, and using, components of or concepts from the various measuring systems and models of excellence, and assembling them into a system which is right for your unit, is also absolutely to be encouraged.

The perfect model or system is the one which contributes most to delivering your own strategic intent.

Personal strategy development

It will not have escaped the reader who has travelled this far through the book that there are great parallels between the strategic process by which organizations prosper and those by which human beings attain fulfilment.

It is entirely appropriate that this last Activity falls in a chapter entitled 'Aspiring to Excellence' for that is another parallel between corporate aspiration and human endeavour.

Try the Activity which follows, first on your own to see what it yields for you. Then perhaps you might wish to involve others whose participation, help and support might fulfil your own strategic intent.

activity

15.1 A personal strategy

Purpose	*Personal*	*Career*

Who are my customers? Who am I serving?

What is my 'product or service'? What am I providing?

What else?

What else?

What is the benefit to my customers of this product/service?

What else?

What else?

Vision

Try the tombstone test; what I'd like to be remembered for.

Complete the following sentence.

Here lies . . . [your name] . . .

who . . .

and who . . .

and who . . .

Values

What three ethical rules can you set yourself that you will never breach?

Another three please.

Strategic intent

Describe a job you would like to be doing now which is consistent with your purpose, consistent with your vision and consistent with your values.

As above but in three years' time.

As above but in ten years' time.

Another approach – complete the following sentence:

When I grow up I'd like to be . . .

Describe personal circumstances which are consistent with your purpose, consistent with your vision and consistent with your values.

Critical success factors
What has to go right to get the job?
And the next two jobs?
What has to go right to create the personal circumstances?

Competencies
What personal changes or personal development is going to be necessary to achieve the CSFs?

Now write up the case study.

Bibliography

The number at the end of each reference indicates the number of the page on which the book is first mentioned.

Goldsmith, W. and Clutterbuck, O. (1997) *The Winning Streak Mark II*, Orion Business Books. (199)

Grove, A. S. (1996) *Only the Paranoid Survive*, Harper Collins. (56)

Hamel, G. and Pralahad, C. *Competing for the Future*, Harvard Business School Press. (59)

Kaplan, R. S. and Norton, D. P. (1996) *The Balanced Scorecard*, Harvard Business School Press. (189)

Levitt, T. (1996) *The Marketing Imagination*, Free Press. (12)

Ohmae, K. (1982) *The Mind of the Strategist*, Penguin. (20)

Peters, T. T. and Waterman, R. H. (1982) *In Search of Excellence*, Warner Books. (199)

Porter, M. E. (1985) *Competitive Advantage: Creating and Sustaining Superior Performance*, Free Press. (16)

Royal Society of Arts (1995) *Tomorrow's Company: The Role of Business in a Changing World*, Royal Society of Arts. (36)

Sun Tzu, (1994) *The Art of War* (edited by Sawyer), Westview Press. (1)

Wellington, P. (1995) *Kaizen Strategies for Customer Care*, Pitman. (31)

Index